Penelopy Tuller Oliveira Freitas
Gustavo Tuller Oliveira Freitas

# AI, HEALTH HAZARDOUS WORK AND RISKS

## Brazil and Florida in Focus

Publisher: Washington & Lincoln University Press
First edition: FEBRUARY 2026 (Revision 1.0)

**Authors:** Penelopy Tuller Oliveira Freitas; Gustavo Tuller Oliveira Freitas.
**Title:** AI, Health Hazardous Work and Risks Brazil and Florida in Focus
**Cover design:** Washington & Lincoln University Press
**Book design:** Washington & Lincoln University Press
**Review:** Washington & Lincoln University Press

**E-book format:** EPUB
**Print format:** Print format: Paperback- 6 x 9 inch

**ISBN:** 978-1-966958-38-3 (Print - Paperback)
**ISBN:** 978-1-966958-37-6 (e-book – EPUB)
**Library of Congress Control Number:** 2026933137


Washington & Lincoln University Press is a division of Washington & Lincoln University, Inc.
Orlando, FL, USA
https://press.walnuniversity.com • https://walnuniversity.com

**Editora:** Washington & Lincoln University Press
**Primeira edição:** fevereiro 2026 (Revisão 1.0)

**Autores:** Penelopy Tuller Oliveira Freitas; Gustavo Tuller Oliveira Freitas.
**Título:** AI, Health Hazardous Work and Risks Brazil and Florida in Focus
**Design da capa:** Washington & Lincoln University Press
**Projeto gráfico:** Washington & Lincoln University Press
**Revisão:** Washington & Lincoln University Press

**Formato e-book:** EPUB
**Formato impresso:** Capa mole - 6 x 9 polegadas

**ISBN:** 978-1-966958-38-3 (Impresso – capa mole)
**ISBN:** 978-1-966958-37-6 (e-book – EPUB)
**Library of Congress Control Number:** 2026933137

Washington & Lincoln University e WALN University são marcas registradas da Washington & Lincoln University, Inc.
Washington & Lincoln University Press é uma divisão da Washington & Lincoln University, Inc.
Orlando, FL, USA
https://press.walnuniversity.com • https://walnuniversity.com

# ACKNOWLEDGMENTS

To God, for his love, goodness, and faithfulness. For allowing me to live out his promises. Lord and Savior of my life. "The Lord has done great things for us, for which we are glad." Psalms 126:3 Thank you for everything, Jesus!

To my parents, whom I love very much, Azemir and Sandra, my eternal gratitude. You taught me, with your examples of strength, dedication and faith, to work hard, to dream and to never give up in the face of difficulties. They have also been with me throughout my career. Thank you for praying for me forever. You are wonderful. I love you more than words can express.

To my brother Gustavo, my great friend and co-author of this book, my admiration, love, affection and gratitude. Your life is a gift to me. Thank you for existing and making everything happier. I love you deeply.

To my love and husband, Eduardo. Thank you for your love and dedication. Thank you for the life partnership. Our story is the most beautiful I know, written by God. Thank you for praying unceasingly for my life and our beautiful family. I love you. How good that we have each other and our beautiful little son. God is too good.

To my son Isaac, my greatest gift, son of promise and reason for my smile. As recorded at Genesis 21:6: "God filled me with laughter, and all those who know about it will laugh with me." You are my greatest blessing, everything with you is very happy. Thank you, my love, for encouraging and vibrating with mom. I loved knowing that you intend to take this book to the literary café of your College, you are really special. I love you very much, my little son.

To Noemia Pereira, my eternal gratitude. Your prayers have been essential in my life. You are a precious person and a true blessing. I love you.

To Lauro and Rose, for their long-standing partnership, since my first steps in Law and Law, almost thirty years ago. I love you, thank you for everything.

To Jose Carlos and Ivani, Leme and Anna, Paulo Piris and Marlene, Vandir and Cathi, Douglas and Fabi, Divo, Lúcia, Marite, Ricardo Massignam — you are very special people, you live in my heart and are part of my trajectory in a unique way. My gratitude for everything they did for me. You are a gift from God in my life. Thank you my dears.

To the friends, professionals and clients of Tuller Freitas Law Office, my second home, for sure, and to everyone who has been there, you are very special.

To Camila Jacobs, Alfredo, Francisco and professors at Ambra University, professionals I deeply admire. You marked my trajectory with your examples of professionalism, dedication, ethics and talent. Thank you so much for your contributions and for being part of this very special moment for me.

To all the teachers I have had throughout my career. My gratitude for the teachings and examples.

To my dear ones from the Christ Water of Life Church in Curitiba, I love you. To my family, my mother-in-law, thank you very much, I love you.

To everyone who, in some way, contributed to the realization of this moment, my sincere gratitude. This book is the result of the efforts, prayers, support, and love of many dear people. May God abundantly bless each one of you, granting you peace, health, success and many achievements.

**Penelopy Tuller Oliveira Freitas**

Thank you, God, for silently guiding me through my professional paths, making me believe in miracles when everything was adversity. Thank you to my parents, always so hard working and dedicated to giving us the best, most of the time taking from themselves, I love you so much. Thank you to my sister, Penelopy, the best lawyer I know, for teaching me how to practice law since the internship, when I was only 17 years old, teaching me about determination ("Gustavo, the opposing party already has a lawyer, find a way out"), for letting me leave her office in 2010 and for inviting me to come back in 2018, when I thought my life had fallen apart forever. For offering me a very ugly room, so that I could also learn about humility and economy, to acquire our beautiful office, I love our little corner, sister, you are amazing. Thank you, Amanda, my sister of the heart, who joined me while still in law school, in 2004, when we were nobody, teaching me about self-acceptance and freshness for food. Thank you for lending me your credit card so many times when cash was an issue. Thank you for letting me know about the applications for the selection process of Instructor Lawyer of the OAB/PR in 2011, a position that I would hold for 3 years before being promoted to Manager of TED/PR, for another 4 years, you changed my life. Thank you for accepting to work with me at the firm since 2022 and for enriching our theses (and creating new ones), with your powerful mind, your peculiar whimsy and zeal, you are wonderful, I love you very much. Thank you Eduardo Mecenas, my brother-in-law, brother at heart and pastor, for so many prayers, revelations and antics. For teaching me about patience, meekness, and faith (although I didn't learn much, but you did). Thank you also for being the father of my beautiful nephew, Isaac, the funniest and smartest little boy planet Earth has ever seen. Thank you, Monica, my little sister with the youngest heart, for relieving the pressure on the difficult days with your immense heart, kindness, easy laughter and optimism, always lying to me about how wonderful I supposedly am and even for helping me in my move, episode in which some belongings fell from the moving truck, inspiring the phrase "there are days that we win and days that we lose and today we will not stop at BR to suffer the humiliation of looking for this crap that flew". Thank you to my friend Géssika, a lawyer with powerful oratory and jokes on the tip of her tongue, for always being a fun company, for infecting me with her wonderful self-esteem, we can't live without you. Thank you to the TED/PR collaborators (2014 to 2018), who stood by me as warriors in the arduous task of migrating the physical processes from TED to electronic ones and for celebrating with me, 2 years after the beginning of this painful process, the result of our management, when we had completed 70% of the processes in progress, thanks to the optimization of everyone's work and effort. Thank you to Dr. Odair Moreschi, at the time General Inspector of the OAB/PR, responsible for the reality shock that we all needed to receive at that moment. For the hard teachings on practicality, effectiveness, speed and for forcing me to become the greatest statistician that TED/PR has ever seen. You are a great example of character and professionalism and, although you may not know it, I carry your image as a teacher to this day in everything I do. Thank you to Dr. Thais Takahashi, my greatest and first motivator to professionally defend fellow lawyers in disciplinary proceedings, for showing me that I am capable, for entrusting me with such important tasks, for teaching me that we can always go further, I am very proud and admired for you. Thank you to Marcelo Woitschecovsky, for the unconditional, and sometimes silent, support in the darkest moments I have lived, I owe you a lot and I will not forget a single day everything you did for me. Thank you to Dr. Davi, lawyer, writer, advisor (the boy doesn't stop), for having worked with us for several years, saving us from the difficult days with his competence and speed, we admire you so much. Thank you to Dr. Giugliana Carta, this encyclopedia in the form of a lawyer, beautiful, charming and fun. Thank you initially for the professional partnership, for believing and trusting me, for teaching me that I don't need to conflict with the adverse party to win, because there is mediation (although I am definitely not fit for the task at hand). Thank you for the dedicated friendship, for the brotherhood built, always fun and funny, even on the most unlikely days. Lost in Manhattan with my feet injured from walking or sitting in a bad bar in Bacacheri, I know I'll have fun and be inspired just by being by your side, thank you for your light and power. Thank you to my favorite PRF (and the most beautiful in the institution), Nilshely, for her friendship, sober advice and for answering calls at dawn, you are very loved and it is a great privilege to always have you with us. Thank you to Dr. Gisele, lawyer, nutritionist, pedagogue and partner of purposeless travel. Thank you for always being there for me and for having so much fun. Thank you to my cousin Paula, for the friendship, coffees, laughter and policing advice. Thank you to my friend Nanci and her husband Euclides, always advising me as parents, but sharing experiences as friends, I love you. Thank you to my psychologist and analyst, Dr. Áurea, for making me see life from the healthiest possible perspective on a weekly basis and for being my almost-friend, since, according to her, analyst and patient cannot be friends. Thank you to my friend and neighbor Karina, for always taking care of my house and my kittens when I'm away, you are a gift. Thank you to my friend and helper Geralda, for keeping my house in habitable condition and for ruining my annual Spotify stat by listening to Alan and Aladin nonstop while you're there. Thank you to my kittens, Breno and Theo, who have not yet learned to read, but need to be mentioned for all the love they dedicate to me, since they have no other option. Thank you to my good friend, Taylor Swift, who doesn't leave the house, for thinking like me and expressing in words what I can't. Thank you to my friends and lawyer clients, who trusted me, despite the break in the standard. And finally, thank you to all those who stood against me on my journey, because I also owe my victories to the transversal encouragement of each one of you, keep following me.

**Gustavo Tuller Oliveira Freitas**

# TABLE OF CONTENTS


Acknowledgments v

About the authors 15

Introduction 17

Contextualization of the Theme 19

The Relevance of the Theme Today 22

The Problem of Unhealthiness in Brazil and the Use of Artificial Intelligence (AI) 26

Fundamentals of Health Hazardous Work in Labor Law 35

Concept of Unhealthiness and its Historical Evolution 35

Regulatory Standards and the CLT 39

Species and Degrees of Unhealthiness 42

Most affected sectors 46

Technical Evidence and Judicial Expertise 48

The Judicialization of Unhealthiness and the Limits of Traditional Expertise 51

Artificial Intelligence in the Workplace 55

What is Artificial Intelligence: Concepts and Applications 55

AI as a Tool for Managing Occupational Risks 60

Predictive Technologies and Smart Sensors 63

Automation of Health Hazardous Tasks: Robots, Algorithms, and Monitoring 64

Benefits of AI in Preventing Harm to Worker Health 67

Artificial Intelligence as Disruptive Innovation 70

Impacts of Artificial Intelligence on Brazilian Labor Justice 75

The Incorporation of Artificial Intelligence in the Labor Courts 75

AI in the Production of Evidence and Prevention of Labor Litigation 77

The Transformation of Forensic Evidence Using Digital Data 79

AI as Support in the Instruction and Judgment of Labor Lawsuits 82

Procedural Efficiency and Reduction of Litigation 84

Ethical and Legal Risks if AI in Labor Justice 87

The Role of the Judiciary in the Face of the Automation of the Work Environment 90

The Role of Labor Law in the Face of Automation 93

The Experience of the Victor System in the Supreme Court 94

Precedent 448, Item II, of the Superior Labor Court 99

Content Provided for in the Precedent Understanding 99

Practical Analysis of Automated Toilets 102

AI Contributions: Automated Toilets 105

Application of AI in the Reduction of Health Hazardous Work 109

Predictive Sensors and Algorithms 111

National/International Case Studies and Experiences 113

The Protection of Workers' Health in Florida (Usa) and the Absence of the Concept of "Unhealthiness" in the Brazilian Sense 117

Overview of Occupational Health and Safety in the United States 117

Enforcement of the Osh Act and Osha Standards in Florida 121

Florida's Own Laws and Policies Related to Occupational Health 124

Guidelines and Programs for Businesses in Florida 127

Artificial Intelligence, Risk Monitoring, and Regulatory Compliance in Florida 130

Conclusion 135

References 141

# ABOUT THE AUTHORS

## *Penelopy Tuller Oliveira Freitas*

Penelopy Tuller Oliveira Freitas – Business Lawyer since 2003. Partner at Tuller Freitas Law Office in Curitiba/PR. Master's student in Business and Technology Law – Risk and Compliance at Washington & Lincoln University. Specialist in Applied Law, Specialist in Tax Management and Legislation, Specialist in Sports Law and Theology.

## *Gustavo Tuller Oliveira Freitas*

Gustavo Tuller Oliveira Freitas – Lawyer in Ethical, Disciplinary and Business matters since 2009. Member of the Tuller Freitas Law Firm in Curitiba/PR. Specialist in Public Law, Specialist in Criminal Law and Criminal Procedure. Author and Co-author of articles, especially in the areas of Disciplinary Ethics.

# INTRODUCTION

The rise of Artificial Intelligence (AI) has caused significant transformations in productive structures and social institutions, with direct impacts on labor relations and occupational risk management models. Among the various challenges faced in the labor environment, health hazardous conditions stand out as a historical factor of illness and violation of workers' fundamental rights. In this context, this work analyzes how the law can be applied as an instrument to reduce unhealthy environments, contributing to the protection of the health and dignity of the human person in the world of work, reducing business costs with the payment of additional remuneration provided for in Brazilian legislation, anticipating risks and contributing to faster judicial decisions. At the same time, it alerts to the ethical, legal and social challenges of automation.

The work also analyzes the North American system of protection of workers' health used in the State of Florida, which has as its central milestone the enactment of the Occupational Safety and Health Act of 1970. This broke with the logic of protection that existed until then and established a national policy aimed at ensuring safe and healthy working conditions through mandatory standards and inspection, structuring the duties of employers and the prevention of occupational accidents and diseases in the United States.

Based on authors such as Schwab (2016) and Harari (2018), it is understood that the Fourth Industrial Revolution has repositioned artificial intelligence as a central element in the reconfiguration of human relations with production. In particular, the replacement of health hazardous tasks with autonomous, algorithmic and robotic operations represents not only a productivity gain, but also a change in the institutional approach to occupational safety and health. Souza (2022) argues that the highest incidence of occupational accidents occurs precisely in sectors with a lower degree of automation, which reinforces the importance of adopting smart technologies for risk prevention.

In this sense, the present study is anchored in an argumentative-descriptive approach to analyze the effects of AI in the reduction of unhealthy work, focusing on sectors such as basic industry, mining, civil construction and urban cleaning services, in which exposure to harmful agents can occur. Technologies such as smart sensors, autonomous robots, and digital monitoring systems have been applied to minimize human presence in adverse conditions, transforming the role of the worker and the employer in the face of labor legislation.

This work also explores the effects of AI in the sphere of Brazilian Labor Justice, with emphasis on its performance on three main fronts: the production of expert evidence, the prevention of litigation and the remote inspection of working conditions. At this point, the contribution of Ferreira (2022) stands out, who, by analyzing the experience of the Victor system in the Federal Supreme Court (Brazil), demonstrates how the law can help in the rationalization of jurisdictional activity, filtering demands and optimizing the procedural process. Although Ferreira's research focuses on the constitutional sphere, his findings are transposable to the universe of the Labor Courts, with the overloads and need for efficient management.

In addition, the use of AI in the inspection of unhealthy conditions in Brazil can represent a qualitative leap in the control of compliance with health and safety standards. Remote inspection and predictive analysis systems allow you to identify risk patterns in advance, enabling the adoption of corrective measures before the occurrence of possible damage to the worker. In this way, AI acts preventively, collaborating for the effective protection of the work environment.

Finally, it is verified that AI, although it does not replace the need for regulation

and human supervision, is an essential tool for promoting a safer and more efficient work environment. The challenge lies in the construction of a legal framework that recognizes the limits and possibilities of technology, ensuring that innovation occurs in line with the fundamental principles of Labor Law and with the social function of employment.

# CONTEXTUALIZATION OF THE THEME

The accelerated advancement of technology, especially with the consolidation of Artificial Intelligence (AI), has caused profound transformations in various sectors of society, especially the world of work. The Fourth Industrial Revolution, as Schwab (2016) points out, is characterized by the convergence of digital, physical, and biological technologies, with AI being one of the most important pillars of this process. In this context, it is essential to analyze how AI is reconfiguring the work environment and, in particular, its role in reducing unhealthy conditions.

Historically, unhealthy environments have always been linked to exposure to physical, chemical, or biological agents that are harmful to the health of workers. Sectors such as mining, civil construction, urban cleaning and basic industry concentrate a large part of the activities classified as unhealthy. According to Souza (2022), "the high incidence of occupational diseases in these sectors is related to the low integration of technological solutions that reduce human exposure" (p.67). Thus, the application of AI emerges as a concrete possibility of positive intervention.

Based on this, several initiatives have been implemented globally with a view to incorporating intelligent systems into production processes. Collaborative robots, predictive algorithms, automated sensors, and decision-making systems based on AI are being used to minimize risks and replace human action in highly dangerous contexts. Harari (2018) emphasizes that "algorithms not only make decisions, but learn from data in real time, offering adaptive and safe responses" (p.132), which makes them allies in preserving life and health in the workplace.

By considering AI as a risk management tool, it is possible to observe its direct impact on the prevention of unhealthy conditions. In activities such as industrial painting, demolition, hospital waste collection and handling of toxic materials, the replacement of human presence by automated mechanisms has generated gains in efficiency and reduction of occupational morbidity. Pagnanelli and Ravasio (2020) highlight that "the implementation of AI in industry 4.0 should be thought of as a structuring axis of occupational health" (p.47), which reinforces the relevance of the theme.

Another relevant aspect is the relationship between AI and labor regulation. Digital transformation is not limited to the productive sphere; it also reaches the justice system, especially the Labor Courts. In this context, technologies based on AI have been used to optimize procedural management and facilitate decision-making. Ferreira (2022) analyzes the experience of the Victor System within the scope of the Federal Supreme Court and states that "artificial intelligence has a real capacity to contribute to jurisdictional efficiency and the rationalization of the procedural acquis" (p.59).

Although the Victor System operates in the STF, its operating logic can be replicated in the Labor Courts, notably in technical expertise, in the management of digital evidence, and in the inspection of working conditions via remote monitoring.

The possibility of using AI to monitor work environments in real time allows for more preventive, decentralized, and efficient action in protecting against health hazard risks.

In addition, the pandemic context accelerated the adoption of smart technologies in all sectors, including legal and labor. The COVID-19 pandemic has exposed the need for tools that ensure the safety of workers, even in harsh conditions. AI, by enabling the automation of essential tasks, has prevented the exposure of thousands of workers to contaminated environments, illustrating its potential in coping with unsanitary conditions.

In this sense, the present work is based on the recognition that the law should be analyzed not only as a technological tool, but as a social and legal phenomenon. The way technologies are introduced and regulated directly affects the fundamental rights of workers. As Schwab points out (2016), "technology by itself is not neutral: its impact depends on the regulatory, political, and cultural context where it is implemented" (p. 93).

Based on this perspective, it is urgent to reflect on the regulatory frameworks that involve the use of AI in work environments and legal institutions. The absence of specific standardization on the use of algorithms in expert analysis can compromise legal certainty.

Another point that deserves to be highlighted is the potential of AI to generate relevant data on environmental conditions. With sensors distributed in industrial spaces, it is possible to build real-time risk maps, with information on temperature, humidity, presence of toxic agents and vibrations. Such data can help companies structure environments, as well as magistrates to support judicial decisions, subsidize audits, and reinforce public policies aimed at risk prevention.

However, the incorporation of the law also poses ethical challenges. The protection of workers' personal data, the transparency of algorithms, and the prevention of discriminatory biases must be treated seriously. The General Data Protection Law (LGPD) establishes important guidelines for the responsible use of information in corporate environments.

Therefore, the debate on AI and health hazards is also a debate on human rights, inclusion and equity in access to technology. The use of AI cannot deepen existing inequalities or justify the indiscriminate replacement of workers by machines. It is necessary to ensure that innovation is accompanied by training, education and social responsibility.

Therefore, the contextualization of the theme reveals the urgency of a new paradigm of analysis of working conditions, in which the law assumes a central, but not absolute, role. Their integration must occur in a complementary way to human work, strengthening the protection of social rights, helping companies and promoting a safer work environment.

According to Ferreira (2022), "AI in the Judiciary does not eliminate the judge, but redefines his function and expands his capacity to manage justice" (p.61). The same logic can be applied to the world of work: AI does not replace the worker, but redefines their role, expands their protection, and helps companies, especially in reducing unhealthy environments.

Finally, it is hoped that this work will contribute to the deepening of discussions about the relationship between technology and occupational health, encouraging the formulation of public policies, regulations and judicial decisions that promote the dignity of work in the era of artificial intelligence.

In addition to the Brazilian panorama, it is pertinent to contextualize the experience of the United States, with a focus on Florida, as a methodological and normative counterpoint. Unlike Brazil – where "health hazardous work" has its own legal meaning, associated with additional remuneration and frequent judicialization – the North American context is organized, as a rule, by a logic of prevention and compliance, centered on technical standards of occupational safety and health, inspection and accountability of the employer.

## THE RELEVANCE OF THE THEME TODAY

It is necessary to keep up with the transformations that Artificial Intelligence (AI) is causing in the dynamics of work, especially with regard to occupational health and safety. In a global scenario marked by the digitalization of processes and intelligent automation, it is essential to investigate how these technologies can contribute to reducing unhealthiness in work environments, particularly in sectors historically exposed to high risks. According to Schwab (2016), the Fourth Industrial Revolution demands a reconfiguration of public policies, legislation and organizational culture so that technological gains revert into concrete social benefits.

Considering this context, there is a need to broaden the academic and institutional debate on the preventive role of AI in labor relations. Although there is a large literature on the economic impacts of automation, there are few studies specifically focused on its ability to promote safer work environments. As Souza (2022, p.72) observes, "discussions about artificial intelligence still focus excessively on the effects of replacing jobs, neglecting its potential as an ally in the protection of occupational health".

Furthermore, the choice for the thematic focus involving unhealthiness is based on the social relevance of the theme. Data from the Observatory of Safety and Health at Work (2021) reveal that Brazil registers an average of more than 500 thousand work accidents per year, many of which result from exposure to unhealthy environments. Thus, investigating technological solutions that can contribute to the mitigation of these risks is an ethical and political requirement that goes beyond the field of innovation.

Another factor that reinforces the relevance of this analysis is the context of the Labor Courts and their relationship with new technologies. The experience of the Victor System in the Federal Supreme Court (STF), as analyzed by Ferreira (2022), demonstrates that the law can be a valuable instrument for the optimization of jurisdictional activity.

According to the author, "the use of algorithms in the Judiciary enables not only greater speed, but also the improvement of the selection of relevant demands" (Ferreira, 2022, p.59). This opens the way for reflections on how similar tools can be adapted to the labor field.

The mechanisms in which AI influences working conditions are analyzed. It is about proposing an integrated approach between Law, Engineering, Health and Technology, in order to elaborate diagnoses and suggest solutions to a real and persistent problem. Harari (2018) points out that "the history of technological revolutions is also the history of conflicts over their appropriation and regulation" (p.138), which indicates the need for a critical position in the face of innovations.

On a practical level, this work seeks to contribute to the improvement of public policies aimed at the prevention of risks at work. The implementation of intelligent sensors, autonomous robots and remote monitoring systems can, if well regulated, serve to support the action of Public Prosecutors, unions and inspection agencies. Likewise, to contribute so that companies can structure healthy environments. In this way, IA not only replaces the human gaze, but enhances it, expanding its capacity to intervene and protect.

Normative paths for responsible regulation of AI in the workplace are proposed. Currently, Brazilian legislation is still moving slowly towards a specific standardization for these tools. As Schwab (2016) reminds us, "regulation needs to keep up with the pace of innovation, otherwise it will become irrelevant or, worse, harmful" (p.121). Labor Law, therefore, must be able to respond to technological challenges based on its founding principles.

From an academic point of view, the theme is interdisciplinary and instigates dialogue between knowledge areas. Studies such as those by Pagnanelli and Ravasio (2020) have already been exploring how the integration between production engineering, ergonomics, and AI can generate safer and more efficient environments. However, there is still an unexplored space for the Law to position itself as a mediator in this process, building guarantees so that the digital transition is also a protective transition.

In the same sense, it is necessary to consider that the debate on unhealthiness is intrinsically linked to the idea of social justice. It is in the most unhealthy jobs that the most vulnerable workers are, in general: with less education, low pay and few opportunities for social mobility. Offering these people technologically safer environments is a way to combat inequality and promote dignity.

In addition, the inclusion of the North American approach, especially from Florida, reinforces the contemporary relevance of the theme by showing that the discussion on unhealthy and occupational health crosses borders and dialogues with global challenges: intensification of environmental risks, productive reorganization, new technologies for surveillance of the work environment and the need for compliance in integrated economic chains.

The choice of the theme also dialogues with the Sustainable Development Goals (SDGs) of the UN 2030 Agenda, especially goals 8 (decent work and economic growth) and 9 (industry, innovation and infrastructure). AI can be an instrument for achieving these goals, as long as it is used responsibly and with respect for fundamental rights.

The application of AI, in turn, needs to be accompanied by technological education and digital inclusion processes. It is not enough to install intelligent machines in work environments; It is necessary to train workers to operate, interpret and question them. Training is the key to preventing technology from becoming a new form of domination.

The Labor Court can also directly benefit from AI-based technologies. Systems for screening cases, organizing case law, cross-referencing data, and predicting legal risks are tools that can bring efficiency without sacrificing the rights of the parties. As Ferreira (2022, p.62) observes,

"AI, when correctly used, frees the judge for the most complex interpretative tasks, optimizing the time and quality of decisions"

For these reasons, the analysis is relevant from both a theoretical and practical point of view. It aims to offer a critical analysis of the role of AI in promoting healthier work environments, without disregarding the risks, regulatory challenges and ethical dilemmas that this technology imposes.

Finally, it is hoped that the results presented here will serve as a subsidy for the elaboration of public policies, guide judicial decisions and inspire new research on the subject. Human work, when protected by intelligent technologies, reaffirms its centrality in the project of society, but also requires a new look on the part of Law and institutions.

Thus, the law should not be seen as an end in itself, but as a means of realizing rights. This is the purpose of this work: to understand how artificial intelligence can stop being just a technological promise and become a concrete tool for social justice and job security.

# THE PROBLEM OF UNHEALTHINESS IN BRAZIL AND THE USE OF ARTIFICIAL INTELLIGENCE (AI)

Unhealthiness, understood as habitual exposure to agents harmful to health in the workplace, represents one of the most persistent challenges of contemporary labor relations. In a country like Brazil, with high rates of accidents and occupational diseases, the search for innovative solutions to reduce these risks is an urgent social need. In this context, the emergence of Artificial Intelligence (AI) as a tool capable of automating processes, predicting risks, and monitoring environmental conditions in real time has generated significant expectations about its application in the promotion of occupational health.

Based on this premise, the present study aims to investigate how AI can contribute to the reduction of unhealthiness in work environments, especially in sectors such as civil construction, mining, urban collection and heavy industry. As Souza (2022) points out, "the performance of AI can replace the worker in repetitive and dangerous tasks, significantly reducing human exposure to harmful agents" (p.75). This perspective is in line with the understanding that technology not only improves productivity, but can also act as an ally in guaranteeing fundamental rights.

In this sense, the research is also guided by the need to understand the impact of AI in the scope of Labor Courts in Brazil. The modernization of the Judiciary, especially through the use of intelligent systems, has been a response to the growing demand for speed, efficiency, and assertiveness in conflict resolution. Ferreira (2022, p.59) analyzes the use of the Victor System in the Federal Supreme Court and states that "the application of the law allows the Judiciary to deal with large volumes of data and identify decision-making patterns, optimizing human work".

Although the Victor System was developed for the STF, its model can be replicated in specialized areas such as the Labor Courts, notably in the analysis of technical expertise, in the organization of jurisprudence and in the monitoring of working conditions. The inspection of unhealthy environments, for example, could be intensified with the use of intelligent sensors and analytical platforms capable of recording deviations in temperature, humidity, noise and the presence of toxic agents, helping companies to structure healthy environments, as well as issuing automatic alerts to those responsible and inspection agencies.

However, it must be recognized that the incorporation of the law into the world of work also raises relevant ethical, legal and institutional issues. The replacement of human labor by machines must be accompanied by professional requalification policies, otherwise social exclusion will deepen and accentuate inequalities. Harari (2018) warns that "automation can generate a new social class: that of disposables, which have lost their economic value" (p. 140).

The research also problematizes the fact that there is, so far, no clear and comprehensive legal framework that regulates the use of LA in work environments. Such absence compromises legal certainty and opens the door to the indiscriminate exploitation of technologies, including to the detriment of workers' rights. According to Schwab (2016), "regulation is as important as innovation; without it, technology can be misused or monopolized" (p. 93).

This question is anchored in the need to understand the relationship between technology, regulation, worker well-being and aid to companies. It is not just about evaluating the operational efficiency of AI, but about investigating its transformative potential in structuring a more humane, fair, and safe work environment. The research seeks, therefore, to overcome the merely instrumental view of technology.

By addressing the impact of the law on the Labor Courts, it is also intended to explore the role of the Judiciary as an agent of social innovation. The ability to integrate data, predict litigation, streamline the procedural process, and support decisions based on empirical evidence positions AI as a strategic tool in promoting social justice.

In this sense, one of the secondary objectives of this research is to understand how AI can collaborate with the performance of the Public Prosecutor's Office of Labor and the Labor Inspection in the identification of health hazardous work conditions in Brazil, even before the occurrence of damage to the worker's health. This requires, of course, investments in technological infrastructure and technical training of the teams involved.

In addition, it is essential to discuss the criteria for admissibility of evidence obtained by AI in labor lawsuits. The chain of custody of data, the auditability of algorithms, and the protection of workers' privacy are elements that need to be carefully analyzed. The General Data Protection Law (Law No. 13,709/2018) offers an initial framework, but there are still gaps to be filled.

Another important point is the need to make the use of the law compatible with the basic principles of Labor Law, such as the dignity of the human person, the appreciation of work and the social function of the company. These principles cannot be relativized in the name of technological innovation. As Ferreira (2022, p.60) points out, "artificial intelligence cannot become a new form of inequality, but must be understood as a mechanism of justice and equity".

This work also dialogues with the urgency of preventive action and not just reparatory action by the legal system. AI, with its predictive analytics capabilities, allows the focus to shift from punishment to prevention, which can result in healthier work environments and a reduction in labor litigation.

Finally, it aims to build paths that promote the ethical, inclusive, and efficient use of AI in the world of work. Not only to understand the limits and potentialities of technology, but also to subsidize the formulation of public policies and normative guidelines that ensure respect for social rights, the full protection of workers' health, as well as to assist companies in structuring healthy environments.

Artificial Intelligence (AI), when applied in an ethical and regulated manner, has the potential to significantly reduce unhealthy work environments, especially in sectors of greater occupational vulnerability, such as mining, construction, heavy industry, and urban cleaning services. This assumption is based on the ability of AI systems to replace human labor in repetitive, dangerous, or unhealthy tasks, in addition to monitoring environmental variables and anticipating risk situations. According to Schwab (2016, p. 104), "intelligent automation will be the key to cleaner, more efficient and safer industrial environments".

In a complementary way, it is hypothesized that AI, when integrated into the practices of the Labor Courts, can improve the mechanisms for inspection, prevention and resolution of disputes involving unhealthy working conditions. Tools such as connected sensors, predictive algorithms, and data analysis systems can provide justice with objective elements to support decisions and guide public policies. According to Ferreira (2022, p.61), "AI can assist in the early detection of labor violations, assist companies in structuring healthy environments, contributing to a more proactive and resolute judicial action"

In this sense, a third hypothesis concerns the possibility of AI contributing to the rationalization of labor litigation, especially in demands related to unhealthy and dangerous work. Currently, many litigations arise from the difficulty of proving working conditions, which could be mitigated with the use of technologies for capturing and continuously recording environmental data. As Souza (2022) points out, "artificial intelligence allows a new way of producing and analyzing evidence, more precise and less subjective" (p.79).

Another relevant hypothesis refers to the impact of AI on the transformation of the organizational culture of companies. It is based on the idea that the adoption of intelligent technologies, when accompanied by ethical guidelines and adequate technical training, can induce a paradigm shift in the management of occupational health and safety. Harari (2018) argues that "technologies not only change what we do, but alter the way we think and relate to the world" (p.144), which suggests an indirect effect of AI on the valuation of working life. In addition, it analyzes how AI can reduce or eliminate unhealthy environments, reduce business costs with the payment of additional remuneration provided for in Brazilian legislation, anticipate risks, and contribute to faster judicial decisions.

It is also hypothesized that the use of AI can make the performance of labor inspection more efficient, especially in view of the limitation of human and material resources of public agencies. Through the automation of inspection processes and the systematic collection of data, it would be possible to expand the coverage and effectiveness of control actions, as well as to assist companies in structuring healthy environments. Pagnanelli and Ravasio (2020) highlight that "the convergence between

AI and safety engineering are promising for the anticipation of occupational risks and for the design of more protective work environments" (p.52).

Within the scope of the Judiciary, it is also supported the hypothesis that the law can assist in the predictive analysis of demands, allowing courts to identify patterns of recurrence of violations and establish preventive strategies. This would imply a transition from reactive justice to predictive and educative justice, in line with the constitutional principles of prevention and dignity of the human person.

Furthermore, the hypothesis is raised that the integration between AI and the databases of the Labor Court can contribute to the construction of sectoral diagnoses on unhealthiness, informing public policies and more focused inspection actions, as well as assisting companies in structuring healthy environments.

As Ferreira (2022, p.63) suggests, "algorithms, by cross-referencing information from processes, expertise, and reports, generate strategic knowledge for the promotion of healthier environments".

AI can collaborate in the construction of more robust technical evidence, reducing the excessive judicialization of expert issues and making the process faster and more efficient. The reliability of the data collected by smart sensors, combined with the traceability of the algorithms used, reinforces the credibility of the evidence presented. It is hypothesized that the law can help companies in structuring healthy environments and foster the objective responsibility of companies in relation to unhealthy conditions, since the technology allows the continuous generation of records about the work environment, making it difficult to claim ignorance or unpredictability regarding exposure to harmful agents.

Another hypothetical point to be considered is the possibility that the law will stimulate the revision of the normative parameters of unhealthiness, currently based on point measurements and fixed tables. Artificial intelligence, by allowing real-time measurements and multivariate analyses, can induce a more accurate and dynamic updating of legislation. Likewise, the hypothesis is formulated that AI, when used in the analysis of epidemiological data on occupational diseases, can anticipate trends and guide more effective occupational health policies, promoting intersectoriality between law, public health and engineering.

It is hypothesized that AI can contribute to the promotion of intergenerational justice, by protecting younger workers from unhealthy environments and preserving their work capacity in the long term. This meets the principles of sustainability and prevention provided for in the Federal Constitution and in international treaties to which Brazil is a signatory. The hypothesis that the la, when applied with transparency and under public governance, can reinforce social trust in institutions, since its results, being auditable and subject to review, confer objectivity and impartiality to judicial and administrative decisions.

Another relevant hypothesis is that the law can promote greater equality of access to justice. Technology can act as a reducer of procedural asymmetries. The present investigation is also based on the hypothesis that the use of the law can positively influence the construction of more uniform jurisprudence on unhealthiness, reducing contradictory decisions and increasing the predictability of the labor court system. Still, it is proposed the hypothesis that the law can stimulate the development of new professional skills, requiring legal operators and inspection institutions to incorporate knowledge in data science, statistics and digital security.

At the political-institutional level, it is defended the hypothesis that the adoption of AI in unhealthy issues can strengthen the legitimacy of the Labor

Courts in society, by demonstrating its capacity for innovation and effective response to contemporary challenges. Another related hypothesis is that the law can favor the integration between the Labor Courts, the Labor Public Prosecutor's Office and regulatory agencies, through the sharing of data and the construction of collaborative platforms to confront unhealthiness.

Finally, it is believed that IA can expand the concept of decent work, by not only preserving the life and health of workers, but also by contributing to smarter, more autonomous and humanized work environments, in line with the UN Sustainable Development Goals. In view of these hypotheses, this work analyzes the limits, possibilities, and impacts of artificial intelligence in the construction of a new culture of risk prevention in the world of work, articulating technological innovation, legal regulation, and social justice.

# FUNDAMENTALS OF HEALTH HAZARDOUS WORK IN LABOR LAW

## CONCEPT OF UNHEALTHINESS AND ITS HISTORICAL EVOLUTION

Health hazardous work, as a labor legal institute, is a category aimed at protecting workers exposed to conditions adverse to their health and safety, which derives from the Latin term unhealthy, which refers to what harms health. In a legal sense, it refers to work activities that impose on the employee habitual contact with physical, chemical, or biological agents capable of causing damage to physical or mental integrity, when the tolerance limits provided for in technical standards are exceeded (Delgado, 2020).

In Brazil, the legal basis for the recognition of unhealthy conditions is found in article 189 of the Consolidation of Labor Laws (CLT), which establishes as such "activities that, by their nature, working conditions or methods, expose employees to agents harmful to health, above the established tolerance limits". Thus, the legal concept of unhealthiness is eminently technical and must be verified by specialized expertise, in order to ensure objectivity in the granting of the respective additional pay (Brazil, 1943).

The historical construction of the notion of unhealthiness is directly linked to the emergence of salaried work in the large industrial cities of the nineteenth century, since, during the Industrial Revolution, workers were subjected to exhausting working hours, closed environments, exposure to heat, noise, toxic substances and lack of ventilation. Such conditions resulted in various occupational diseases, such as pneumoconiosis, chronic poisoning and physical injuries

(Dejours, 2011).

At first, the relationship between work and illness was treated empirically, without state regulation. The growth of workers' struggles gave rise to the first labor laws in Europe, such as the Factory Acts, which already provided for limitations on work in unhealthy environments, whose context influenced the emergence of labor law as an autonomous and protective branch (Antunes, 2020).

In Brazil, the recognition of occupational diseases and unhealthiness as an object of legal protection began to take shape in the 1930s and 1940s, especially with the creation of the Ministry of Labor and the enactment of the CLT in 1943. Although the CLT already mentioned unhealthiness, the absence of technical parameters made it difficult to apply it effectively, and judicial expertise was one of the only means of investigation (Brazil, 1943).

It was only with the publication of Ordinance No. 3,214/78 of the Ministry of Labor that a robust normative system for the technical characterization of health hazardous work was consolidated, whose ordinance instituted the Regulatory Standards, especially NR-15, which specifically deals with health hazard activities and operations, stipulating tolerance limits for various agents and establishing the criteria for expert evaluation (Brazil, 1978).

The evolution of the concept of health hazardous work is closely linked to the advancement of medical sciences and safety engineering, and occupational medicine and occupational hygiene began to offer technical subsidies for the identification of health risks in work environments. According to Schiavi (2022), the law began to incorporate this knowledge to ensure more objective and technically supported decisions.

From the Federal Constitution of 1988, the protection of workers' health gained a new legal level, being elevated to the category of fundamental right and, thus, article 7, item XXII, began to enshrine the "reduction of risks inherent to work" as a duty of the employer, which includes facing unhealthy conditions through preventive measures, protection engineering and supply of adequate equipment (Brazil, 1988).

Over the years, the concept of health hazardous work has ceased to be restricted to visible physical risks and has started to incorporate invisible chemical agents, microorganisms and, more recently, psychosocial factors. Diseases such as burnout, panic syndrome, and depression related to the work environment have been progressively recognized as forms of occupational illness in unhealthy contexts (WHO, 2022).

This broadening of the concept imposes on labor law the challenge of adapting to new forms of precariousness, and the intensification of the pace of work, the fragmentation of working hours and the abusive use of control technologies are among the factors that, although not chemical or biological, directly impact the health of workers and should be considered in the reformulation of protection norms (Antunes, 2018).

The historical evolution of unhealthy conditions also reflects cultural transformations in the way the value of human work is perceived, since, initially seen as an acceptable burden in the name of economic progress, exposure to risks began to be questioned in the name of the dignity of the human person and the social function of work, principles enshrined in the current constitutional order (Brazil, 1988).

The recognition of unhealthiness as a factor of structural inequality in labor relations led to the formulation of public policies aimed at inspection, such as the performance of labor inspectors, and the adoption of mandatory preventive measures by companies and, thus, programs such as the PGR (Risk Management Program) and the CIPA (Internal Commission for the Prevention of Accidents) are developments of this trajectory (MPT, 2022).

From a legal point of view, the evolution of the institute of health hazardous work has consolidated the right to receive the respective bonus, with salary nature, incidence on vacations, 13th salary, FGTS and social security reflexes.

Precedent 139 of the TST expressly recognizes the repercussion of the unhealthy allowance on other labor funds, which reaffirms its importance in the legal system (TST, 2023).

Taking into account the above, the concept of unhealthiness in the world of work is legally defined as the worker's exposure to agents harmful to health above the tolerance limits established in regulatory standards. In the Brazilian legal system, unhealthy conditions are regulated mainly by Regulatory Standard No. 15 of the Ministry of Labor and Employment (MTE), which establishes the technical criteria for the characterization of unhealthy conditions.

According to Souza (2022, p. 77), "unhealthiness is directly related to the intensity, frequency, and duration of exposure to physical, chemical, or biological agents that exceed the parameters defined by the science of occupational hygiene". Thus, the legal definition of unhealthiness rests on technical bases that require expert measurement, involving environmental measurements and specific laboratory analyses.

In this area, when continuing the debate, it is essential to highlight that the concept of unhealthiness is not fixed, but evolves according to scientific advances and transformations in the production process, which implies that the standards must be continuously reviewed to reflect the reality of the world of work. Ferreira (2022, p.61) argues that "technological transformations impose a constant reassessment of normative parameters, so that the worker's right to health is not emptied by the obsolescence of technical standards". This observation is in line with the criticism of Souza (2022), who points out that the absence of periodic updating of the NRs can lead to the naturalization of health hazards as a structural condition of the work environment, relieving the employer of responsibility and making the worker's suffering invisible.

Understanding health hazardous conditions, therefore, requires a multidisciplinary approach that involves both legal and technical-scientific knowledge, especially in the area of health and occupational safety engineering, whose intersection of knowledge is fundamental to ensure the effective protection of the worker and to ensure that expert reports are aligned with current standards.

Ferreira (2022, p.59) explains that "the legal recognition of unhealthiness depends on the existence of technical evidence that attests to the employee's exposure to aggressive agents on a habitual and permanent basis". This habituality is essential for the characterization of the right to the unhealthy bonus, as provided for in article 189 of the Consolidation of Labor Laws (CLT), which demonstrates that the mere existence of the unhealthy agent is not enough: it is necessary to prove continuous and significant contact with the risk factor.

In this scenario, it is necessary to consider that the identification of unhealthy agents occurs through technical-normative criteria based on tolerance limits established in nationally and internationally recognized standards, whose limits consider the exposure time, the intensity of the agent and the possibility of damage to health.

As Souza (2022, p. 79) points out, the technical characterization of unhealthiness must be carried out in the light of up-to-date scientific parameters, under penalty of judicial decisions detached from the epidemiological reality. Compliance with these criteria is essential to ensure legal certainty in decisions involving unhealthy work allowances and, in addition, Ferreira (2022) warns that the employer's failure to adopt corrective measures or provide adequate personal protective equipment (PPE) can aggravate the worker's exposure and result in civil and administrative liability.

## REGULATORY STANDARDS AND THE CLT

The Regulatory Standards (NRs) and the Consolidation of Labor Laws (CLT) form the legal foundation of safety and health in the Brazilian labor environment and, while the CLT establishes the general principles and legal provisions on the employment contract, the NRs technically detail the requirements related to safety, hygiene and occupational medicine, creating a complementary and essential set of norms for the protection of the worker (Delgado, 2020).

The creation of the Regulatory Standards took place through Ordinance No. 3,214/78, of the then Ministry of Labor, based on article 200 of the CLT, which gives the agency the competence to regulate issues of occupational safety and medicine. This ordinance initially established 28 NRs, a number that expanded over time, reflecting the need to technically discipline the various environments and occupational risks (Brazil, 1978).

Article 157 of the CLT imposes on the employer the duty to comply with and enforce the rules of occupational safety and medicine, while article 158 provides for the obligations of the employee regarding the observance of these rules. This normative balance between employers' duties and workers' obligations is reinforced by the NRs, which detail procedures, preventive measures, and limits of tolerance to harmful agents (Brazil, 1943).

Regulatory Standard No. 15, for example, deals specifically with unhealthy activities, establishing criteria for the characterization of unhealthiness and the respective additional due, based on scientific parameters such as the tolerance limits defined by international organizations, such as the ACGIH. The existence of this NR allows the application of article 189 of the CLT to be applied (Schiavi, 2022).

Allied to this, there is NR-9, which establishes the Environmental Risk Prevention Program (PPRA), required for all companies. The PPRA aims to anticipate, recognize, evaluate and control environmental risks in the workplace, being an essential instrument for the realization of the rights provided for in articles 7, XXII and 225 of the Federal Constitution (Brazil, 1988).

The relationship between NRs and the CLT is one of technical complementarity, as the CLT provides the legal basis, while NRs operationalize this basis through technical specifications. As Leite (2023) observes, this normative structure reflects an attempt to give concreteness to the protection of the health and physical integrity of the worker, taking into account the particularities of each economic activity.

It cannot be overlooked that the regulatory norms are built with tripartite participation: government, employers and workers, and this democratic model strengthens the legitimacy of the NRs and ensures that the regulations reflect the reality of the world of work. According to the International Labor Organization (ILO), social participation in the formulation of standards is essential for the effectiveness of OSH policies (ILO, 2019).

Failure to comply with the NRs may generate administrative, civil and labor penalties, so that the company that does not adopt the measures provided for in the rules may be fined by the labor inspectorate and also be liable for damage to the worker's health, based on articles 186 and 927 of the Civil Code, and article 7, item XXVIII, of the Constitution (Brazil, 2002).

Labor jurisprudence recognizes the normative effectiveness of NRs and, more specifically in relation to the Superior Labor Court (TST), it considers regulatory standards as a technical reference in assessing the employer's liability in cases of accident or occupational disease. Precedent 364 of the TST, for example, deals with hazard pay based on specific NRs (TST, 2023).

It is important to highlight that the NR are subject to review and update according to technical advances and changes in labor relations, and since 2019, the federal government has initiated a normative review process, which has raised concerns about the possible flexibility of worker protection (Antunes, 2018).

NR-1, which deals with general provisions and Occupational Risk Management (GRO), has undergone important changes, consolidating itself as a milestone in the integrated management of health and safety at work, whose standard requires the preparation of the PGR (Risk Management Program), replacing the old PPRA provided for in NR-9, which demonstrates the continuous evolution of the normative system

(Brazil, 2020).

The CLT has also evolved in line with social and technical transformations: the labor reform promoted by Law No. 13,467/2017 amended relevant provisions, but kept intact the provisions on occupational safety and health, reaffirming their unavailable and non-waivable nature. Thus, the norms for the protection of workers' health continue to be under the cloak of the unavailability of fundamental rights (Delgado, 2020).

NRs also play a crucial role in the prevention of accidents, since, according to data from the Observatory of Safety and Health at Work, most serious accidents could be avoided by complying with the standards, which demonstrates that the problem is not in the absence of legislation, but in the ineffectiveness of its practical application (MPT, 2022).

To ensure the effectiveness of NRs, it is essential to strengthen labor inspection, so that the performance of labor inspectors, provided for in article 626 of the CLT, is the main way to control compliance with regulatory standards (Brazil, 2023).

# SPECIES AND DEGREES OF UNHEALTHINESS

Unhealthiness in Brazilian Labor Law is classified according to the types of harmful agents to which workers are exposed, whose categorization allows a more precise technical and legal analysis of occupational risks and the corresponding financial compensation through the unhealthy bonus. As established by Regulatory Standard No. 15 (NR-15), unhealthiness is divided according to the nature of the agent: physical, chemical or biological (Brazil, 1978).

Unhealthy agents present in work environments are classified into three main categories: physical, chemical and biological, as established by Regulatory Standard No. 15 of the Ministry of Labor and Employment (MTE), and each of these categories has specific evaluation criteria, considering the potential effects on the worker's health. Souza (2022, p.83) observes that "physical agents encompass factors such as excessive noise, heat, ionizing radiation, and vibrations, whose prolonged exposure can generate hearing, cardiovascular, and neurological damage*, whose risks are often underestimated in productive environments with low supervision or the absence of effective prevention policies, which requires greater attention from authorities and managers.

Physical agents comprise factors such as noise, vibration, ionizing and non-ionizing radiation, excessive heat and cold, as well as abnormal pressures, and these elements, when they exceed the tolerance limits established by technical standards (such as those of the ACGIH), characterize unhealthy activity. For example, workers in the construction and metallurgical industry are often exposed to continuous noise above 85 decibels, which constitutes medium degree of unhealthiness, according to NR-15 (Schiavi, 2022).

In the field of physical agents, noise is perhaps the most common and underreported element in work environments, so that continuous exposure to noise levels above 85 decibels, especially in shifts longer than eight hours, can irreversibly compromise hearing, in addition to affecting the concentration, sleep and mental health of the worker.

Ferreira (2022, p.70) points out that "noise, when constant and excessive, should be treated as an invisible risk factor, as its damage is not always noticeable in the short term, but accumulates devastating effects over time". The negligence regarding the control of this physical agent evidences an institutional failure that, in addition to the technique, requires legal accountability and adequate reparation to the worker, as provided for in the current legislation and in the labor doctrine.

Exposure to extreme temperatures is also a form of physical unhealthiness that is quite recurrent in several sectors, especially in civil construction, steel, meatpacking and agriculture. Excessive heat can cause dehydration, heat stroke, cardiovascular disorders, and even death from exhaustion, while extreme cold compromises circulation and increases the risk of rheumatological diseases.

Souza (2022, p.85) states that "extreme thermal variations, when not mitigated by adequate breaks, hydration, and specific clothing, constitute a direct violation of the right to health and a safe work environment", while Ferreira (2022) argues that, despite the legal provisions on thermal tolerance limits, many companies still neglect such parameters, either due to lack of technical knowledge or a deliberate option to cut operating costs, which has important legal consequences.

Chemical agents, on the other hand, cover toxic substances absorbed by the respiratory, dermal or oral route, such as solvents, heavy metals, mineral dust, vapors and gases. Exposure to benzene, lead, asbestos, or silica, even at low concentrations, can be extremely harmful, and in these cases, the legislation provides for varying degrees of unhealthiness, depending on the toxicity of the agent and the time of exposure (Delgado, 2020).

They pose a serious risk to workers' health, especially in the sectors Industrial, laboratory, cleaning and agro-industry: products such as solvents, acids, heavy metals, toxic dusts and pesticides have a cumulative effect on the body, and can cause from allergic reactions to occupational cancers. According to Ferreira (2022, p.72), "exposure to chemical substances must be controlled through engineering and administrative measures and the appropriate use of PPE, but these requirements are often neglected".

The invisible nature of chemical hazards makes it difficult to perceive them immediately and requires systematic and technical monitoring by employers. Souza (2022) adds that the assessment of chemical exposure should consider the environmental concentration and toxicity of the substance, as well as the worker's time spent in the contaminated environment.

In turn, biological agents are present mainly in hospital environments, laboratories, garbage collection services, sewage and morgues and, in this way, workers exposed to viruses, bacteria, fungi and other pathogens can develop serious diseases such as hepatitis, tuberculosis and leptospirosis. NR-15 recognizes these activities as unhealthy to the maximum degree, especially when they involve direct contact with patients or contaminated materials (Brazil, 1978).

In addition to the classification by agents, the legislation also defines the degrees of unhealthiness: minimum (10%), medium (20%) and maximum (40%), applied to the minimum wage of the region, as provided for in article 192 of the CLT. This gradation corresponds to the intensity of the exposure and the harmful potential of the agents, and the determination of the degree must be made by means of a technical expert report, based on the tables contained in NR-15 (Brazil, 1943).

Minimal unhealthiness usually involves lower risk exposures, with less aggressive agents or intermittent exposure. An example would be the occasional handling of low-toxicity substances in environments with adequate ventilation and, in these cases, even if the risks are controlled, the additional is guaranteed by law (Leite, 2023).

Medium degree unhealthiness refers to continuous exposure to agents with moderate potential to cause damage: situations such as operating noisy machinery, contact with mineral dust or working under intense heat fall into this category. The additional 20% seeks to compensate for the constant risk to which the worker is subjected (Delgado, 2020).

Maximum unhealthiness is reserved for high-risk activities, whose agents have a high capacity to cause irreversible health problems. This is the case, for example, of nurses in intensive care units, X-ray operators, professionals who handle hospital waste or workers in untreated sewage, so that, in these cases, the law establishes an additional 40% in these cases (Brazil, 1978).

The recognition of the type and degree of unhealthiness is not given by presumption. According to the consolidated case law of the Superior Labor Court, it is essential to carry out a technical examination by a qualified professional who evaluates the work environment and the agents present. Precedent 80 of the TST reinforces this requirement, ensuring legal certainty and technical accuracy (TST, 2023).

Although NR-15 provides an exemplifying list of unhealthy activities, the evaluation must also consider updated parameters of occupational medicine and safety engineering. Technical standards from Fundacentro, Anvisa, and

ACGIH are commonly used as a subsidiary reference in the characterization of degrees of unhealthiness (MPT, 2022).

The legislation provides that the payment of the unhealthy bonus can be eliminated or reduced if the employer implements collective protection measures or provides effective Personal Protective Equipment (PPE). The case law of the TST is firm in requiring that the effectiveness of these PPEs be proven, under penalty of maintaining the right to the additional payment (TST, 2023).

The classification of species and degrees of unhealthiness also has social security repercussions. Working time in unhealthy conditions can guarantee the worker the right to special retirement, provided that there is documentary and technical proof of exposure to harmful agents, as disciplined in article 57 of Law No. 8,213/91 (Brazil, 1991).

It is important to note that the criteria for setting the degree of unhealthiness are eminently technical and are not to be confused with painful or dangerous working conditions, even if these are sometimes present simultaneously, and it is certain that the jurisprudence prohibits the accumulation of unhealthy and dangerous bonuses under the terms of Precedent 364 of the ST, and the worker is allowed to choose the most advantageous (TST, 2023).

In recent times, the advancement of environmental monitoring and occupational risk control technologies has allowed greater precision in the assessment of exposure levels and, thus, methods such as acoustic dosimetry, thermohygrometric evaluation and sampling of chemical agents have been incorporated into technical expertise, which contributes to a fairer characterization of the degrees of unhealthiness (Schiavi, 2022).

## Most affected sectors

The discussion about the sectors most affected by unhealthy conditions requires a detailed approach to economic activities whose operational nature implies the constant exposure of workers to harmful agents, so that one of the most critical sectors is mining, in which employees are subjected to underground environments, mineral dust, excessive heat, vibrations and toxic gases. Ferreira (2022, p.75) states that "mining brings together multiple simultaneous risk factors, which makes its workers particularly vulnerable to severe occupational diseases, such as silicosis and noise-induced deafness".

In addition, the difficulty of access and the depth of the mines make it difficult to implement effective protection measures, which further aggravates the situation of vulnerability. Souza (2022) reinforces that inspection in remote mining areas is limited, which facilitates non-compliance with the rules and perpetuates the cycle of institutional negligence.

Based on this reality, another sector that has a high incidence of unhealthiness is civil construction, marked by operations that expose workers to physical agents such as cement dust, intense noise and extreme temperatures. Souza (2022, p.86) points out that "work on construction sites, often in the open air and with long working hours, significantly increases the risks of respiratory, musculoskeletal, and dermatological diseases".

In addition, the processes of digging, demolition, and transporting heavy materials increase the chances of serious accidents and continuous exposure to harmful chemicals. Ferreira (2022) adds that the degree of informality that still predominates in part of the sector compromises the effectiveness of prevention policies, since many workers do not even have access to adequate personal protective equipment.

Another sector equally vulnerable to the effects of unhealthy conditions is urban cleaning, especially in activities related to solid waste collection, sweeping of public roads and maintenance of public areas. Workers in this area face constant exposure to biological agents such as viruses, bacteria and fungi, as well as chemical risks from industrial and hospital waste disposed of improperly.

Ferreira (2022, p.77) points out that "urban collection should be recognized as one of the activities with the highest degree of exposure to unhealthy agents, especially when carried out without the adequate supply of PPE and without compliance with safety protocols". The social invisibility of this category aggravates the situation, as it hinders the formulation of effective public policies aimed at their protection and in this sense, Souza (2022) reinforces that urban cleaning workers often operate in precarious conditions, with low institutional recognition, which contributes to the perpetuation of highly degrading environments.

Agriculture, especially in its intensive aspect, also stands out among the sectors with the highest incidence of unhealthiness, mainly due to the handling of pesticides, long hours under sun exposure and contact with biological agents present in the soil and plants. Souza (2022, p.88) states that "rural workers, especially those who work in extensive crops, are among the most exposed to toxic risks, often without adequate monitoring of their occupational health".

The absence of frequent inspection in rural regions, combined with the informality in hiring and the scarcity of information on occupational risks, severely compromises health protection. Ferreira (2022) adds that, although there are regulations aimed at rural areas, such as NR-31, their application is often neglected by medium and small companies and producers.

# TECHNICAL EVIDENCE AND JUDICIAL EXPERTISE

The finding of unhealthiness in the work environment requires, by law, the performance of expert technical evidence and, according to article 195 of the Consolidation of Labor Laws (CLT), the characterization and classification of unhealthiness depend on an expert report prepared by an occupational physician or occupational engineer duly qualified under the terms of the current legislation (Brazil, 1943).

Judicial expertise is, therefore, the main technical-legal instrument for determining the existence and degree of unhealthiness. This requirement arises from the complexity of the matter, which requires specific scientific knowledge for the identification of harmful agents, analysis of the intensity of exposure and comparison with the tolerance limits set by regulatory standards, notably NR-15 (Brazil, 1978).

The jurisprudence of the Superior Labor Court is undisputed in the sense that the technical expertise constitutes essential evidence for the analysis of the request for additional unhealthiness, which is why Precedent No. 80 of the TST provides that the elimination of unhealthiness by means of protective measures must be ascertained in an expert examination carried out in the workplace, reinforcing the technical and empirical character of the evidence (TST, 2023).

The appointment of the expert is the responsibility of the labor judge, who must observe the criteria of the Code of Civil Procedure and Resolution No. 132/2011 of the CSJT and, in this sense, the professional must have technical qualification and functional independence to ensure impartiality in the preparation of the report. Expert impartiality is a prerequisite for the validity of evidence, and the expert can be replaced at any time in case of suspicion or impediment (Garcia, 2021).

Pursuant to article 473 of the Code of Civil Procedure, the expert report must present an objective response to the questions formulated by the parties and by the court, clearly indicating the technical grounds used, whose analysis must contemplate not only the existence of the unhealthy agent, but also its concentration, frequency of exposure and the effectiveness of the protective equipment provided (Brazil, 2015).

In addition to the report, the parties may appoint technical assistants and formulate questions, as provided for in articles 465 and 466 of the CPC and, in this sense, the technical assistant is an essential figure to the adversary in the production of technical evidence, acting as a counterpoint to the expert appointed by the court. Although it is not impartial, its opinion can decisively influence the conviction of the magistrate (Leite, 2023).

The characterization of unhealthiness does not necessarily require proof of actual damage to health, but rather habitual exposure to harmful agents above the legal limits, which demonstrates the preventive nature of the rule and, within this focus, expert evidence seeks to assess this exposure in technical terms, without the need for the worker to demonstrate the occurrence of concrete injury (Delgado, 2020).

The effectiveness of the Personal Protective Equipment (PPE) provided by the employer must also be evaluated during the examination, considering that the mere provision of PPE does not exempt the payment of the additional PPE, if it is proven that it is inadequate, ineffective or that it is not used. Forensic analysis is essential to verify the effective neutralization of the unhealthy agent (MPT, 2022).

It is important to emphasize that the technical evidence must observe the principles of adversarial and full defense and, therefore, the report must be presented at least in advance for the parties to manifest themselves, who may contest the content, request clarifications or even a new expert opinion, if they point out relevant defects (Garcia, 2021). There are hypotheses in which technical evidence may be waived, such as in cases where the legal framework of the unhealthy activity is presumed, by virtue of a provision in a collective agreement or in situations already settled in case law. Even so, the general rule is the need for expert production, in order to ensure legal certainty in the setting of the additional (Leite, 2023).

Expert evidence also serves as an instructive element in social security proceedings, especially in lawsuits that seek the recognition of special service time. In these cases, the technical report may support the classification of the activity as special, as provided for in article 58 of Law No. 8,213/91 and in Decrees No. 3,048/99 and No. 4,882/03 (Brazil, 1991).

The specialization of the expert is an element that adds quality to the evidence, because, although the legislation only requires that the expert be a physician or occupational engineer, courts have valued professionals with additional certifications in occupational hygiene and with experience in the specific area of the activity examined. This appreciation is in line with the principles of efficiency and full protection of workers' health (Schiavi, 2022).

# THE JUDICIALIZATION OF UNHEALTHINESS AND THE LIMITS OF TRADITIONAL EXPERTISE

The judicialization of unhealthy conditions has become a recurring reality in the Brazilian labor courts, as workers have more frequently started to claim recognition of the additional amount provided for in article 192 of the CLT. The increase in lawsuits involving unhealthy conditions reflects not only the persistence of inadequate work environments, but also the limits of administrative regulation and on-site inspections promoted by the Ministry of Labor (Delgado, 2020).

This phenomenon of judicialization is fueled by two main factors: on the one hand, the absence of effective preventive control mechanisms in companies; on the other hand, the legal uncertainty regarding the interpretation and application of the Regulatory Standards, especially NR-15, the consequence of which is the overload of the Judiciary with actions whose decision-making core depends, fundamentally, on specialized expert evidence (Leite, 2023).

Judicial expertise, although provided for as a technical means of determining unhealthiness, faces a series of structural and methodological limitations. The traditional model of expertise adopted in the Labor Courts often does not account for the complexity of modern work environments, nor does it adequately address emerging psychosocial risks, such as chronic stress, burnout, and organizational pressures (Schiavi, 2022).

One of the main limitations of traditional forensic examination is its dependence on a single technical visit to the workplace, usually on a scheduled date and with the presence of the employer, which can generate artificial or manipulated conditions, the limitation of which compromises the fidelity of the diagnosis, as it does not capture routine variations and critical moments of the working day (Garcia, 2021).

In addition, the time limitation of the expert opinion prevents the collection of continuous data on occupational exposure, compromising the accuracy of the conclusion. The lack of long-term environmental monitoring equipment, such as individual dosimeters and air samplers, reduces the ability of forensics to reliably measure harmful agents, especially chemical and biological agents (MPT, 2022).

Another critical point lies in the heterogeneous technical training of judicial experts and, although the CLT requires them to be occupational physicians or engineers, many work with little familiarity with certain industrial areas or with the new international occupational hygiene parameters (Delgado, 2020).

The judicialization of unhealthiness also reveals the epistemological limits of traditional expertise, which tends to prioritize physically measurable factors to the detriment of organizational and subjective aspects of work. It should not be forgotten that situations of high mental load, long working hours and hierarchical pressures, even if not visible, are real causes of occupational illness and should be considered in the expert diagnosis (Antunes, 2018).

Expert action sometimes disregards contextual elements, such as the intermittent use of Personal Protective Equipment (PPE), failures in its maintenance, lack of training and organizational resistance to its implementation and, although the supply of PPE is a cause of mischaracterization of unhealthiness, this neutralization must be effective and continuous, under penalty of evading the worker's right (TST, 2023). In addition, it is observed that many magistrates, because they do not master the technical aspects involved, fully adhere to the expert report, even if it is laconic or silent on essential elements. Within this approach, jurisprudence, although recognizing the probative value of expert opinions, admits its relativization through robust technical evidence to the contrary, such as opinions from technical assistants or new expert reports (Leite, 2023).

The judicialization of unhealthiness could be mitigated with greater preventive inspection by the State, as well as with the creation of extrajudicial mechanisms for verifying work environments, such as compulsory technical audits and periodic certifications. The absence of these tools makes the Judiciary the main, and often the only, instance of recognition of rights related to occupational health (MPT, 2022).

There is also a need for normative evolution, since NR-15, for example, despite its historical importance, lacks substantial updates to contemplate new agents and contemporary labor practices. Technological advances and transformations in the world of work require a more comprehensive, interdisciplinary expert model oriented to the integral protection of health (Schiavi, 2022).

The use of digital technologies, such as continuous exposure sensors, environmental monitoring platforms, and artificial intelligence applied to ergonomic analysis, can significantly increase the accuracy of forensic examinations and offer the Judiciary more reliable support for decision-making. Traditional expertise, without these resources, tends to perpetuate structural limitations and outdated interpretations (Antunes, 2018).

It should also be noted that the judicialization of unhealthiness and the limits of traditional expertise reveal a gap between the real complexity of the work and the legal and technical instruments available for its analysis. Overcoming this mismatch requires a new expert paradigm, based on an interdisciplinary, participatory approach anchored in constitutional principles, such as the dignity of the human person and the social valorization of work (Brazil, 1988).

# ARTIFICIAL INTELLIGENCE IN THE WORKPLACE

## WHAT IS ARTIFICIAL INTELLIGENCE: CONCEPTS AND APPLICATIONS

The understanding of Artificial Intelligence (AI) as the protagonist of the Fourth Industrial Revolution requires, first of all, the recognition of its historicity, its theoretical construction, and its consolidation as a disruptive tool. The term "artificial intelligence" was formalized by John McCarthy in 1956, during the Dartmouth Conference, which marked the beginning of systematic research in the area and, since then, AI has gone through different phases of enthusiasm and disappointment until it reached the current stage of technological maturity. According to Schwab (2016, p.18), "the Fourth Industrial Revolution is characterized by the fusion of technologies that are blurring the lines between the physical, digital, and biological spheres."

Previous revolutions were based on mechanization, electricity, and computing, while the Fourth Industrial Revolution is marked by cyber-physical systems that learn, interact, and make decisions, and AI, in this context, is not just a set of programmable algorithms, but a field of knowledge that integrates machine learning, neural networks, natural language processing, computer vision and expert systems. Harari (2018, p.147) points out that "algorithms are becoming the new masters of information, capable of understanding patterns with precision superior to the human mind".

The consolidation of LA as a base technology must be understood as part of a broader process of digital transformation that directly impacts the world of work. Intelligent machines are replacing human labor in repetitive and dangerous tasks, promoting increased productivity and redefining the division of labor between humans and autonomous systems. Therefore, Souza (2022, p.82) states that "artificial intelligence not only improves production efficiency, but also reorganizes the logic of the work process and the management of the workforce".

In this sense, AI represents a paradigmatic break with previous industrial models, since, if in the Second Industrial Revolution human work was centered on physical effort and, in the Third, on the control of computer systems, the Fourth Revolution shifts the role of the worker to cognitive, interpretative and strategic activities. Pagnanelli and Ravasio (2020, p.51) observe that "AI-based automation radically alters the concept of operation, replacing mechanical execution with autonomous decision-making".

The impact of this change is not homogeneous, since sectors with high occupational risk have benefited from the incorporation of intelligent technologies, especially because they allow the removal of workers from unhealthy environments. Collaborative robots, drones, and autonomous sensors have been used in the chemical, mining, and construction industries to reduce human exposure to toxic agents, noise, heat, and vibration. Schwab (2016, p.109) reinforces that "the integration between robotics, lA, and the Internet of Things is creating autonomous and resilient production systems".

The speed of technological change imposes a considerable theoretical and normative challenge on Labor Law: AI not only transforms the modes of production, but also imposes a reassessment of classic legal concepts, such as subordination, working hours, dangerousness, and unhealthiness. As Ferreira (2022, p.59) points out, "the expansion of artificial intelligence in productive environments requires a review of the traditional labor protection logic, based on the centrality of human labor as a productive unit."

From this perspective, AI assumes an ambivalent role: on the one hand, it enhances decent working conditions by reducing environmental risks; on the other hand, it imposes new forms of surveillance, control and precariousness, if its implementation occurs without adequate regulation. Harari (2018) warns that "emerging technologies can become mechanisms of domination if they are not accompanied by robust ethical and legal frameworks" (p. 149).

From a technical point of view, current AI is mostly based on supervised learning models, in which algorithms are trained with large volumes of data to perform specific tasks with high precision, whose characteristic allows its application in medical diagnoses, facial recognition, financial forecasts, and also in the prevention of occupational accidents. As Souza (2022, p.84) exemplifies, "in industrial environments, AI-based sensors are capable of predicting mechanical failures and detecting sudden changes in environmental conditions that indicate risk."

The transition to AI-assisted productive environments requires investments in infrastructure, technical training, and cultural changes in organizations, and it is certain that, today, resistance to automation is still significant in traditional sectors, motivated both by economic uncertainties and by fear of unemployment. However, studies show that AI does not eliminate jobs indiscriminately, but redefines tasks and creates new occupational profiles. Schwab (2016, p.121) adds that "the professions of the future will require digital skills, critical thinking and the ability to adapt to intelligent systems*.

The application of AI in the justice system contributes to addressing structural problems, such as slowness, procedural congestion and limited access to justice for vulnerable workers. The automation of administrative tasks frees up human resources for interpretive activities that require social and legal sensitivity. Souza (2022, p.86) points out that "AI can act as a mediator of justice, as long as it is guided by constitutional values and the principle of human dignity".

AI, therefore, must be understood as a tool for the structural transformation of institutions and not only as a technical innovation, whose incorporation requires a review of protocols, procedural norms, and forms of training for Law and Engineering professionals. Pagnanelli and Ravasio (2020, p.55) suggest that "the training of legal operators should include digital skills and knowledge about intelligent systems as a condition for the ethical and efficient use of technology.

In this regard, it should be noted that Artificial Intelligence (AI) is an area of computer science focused on the development of systems capable of simulating intelligent human behaviors. In its most elementary definition, AI refers to the ability of machines, programs, and algorithms to perform tasks that, until then, would require human intelligence, such as reasoning, learning, perception, and decision-making (Russell & Norvig, 2020).

The term "artificial intelligence" was officially coined at the Dartmouth conference in 1956 by John McCarthy and other researchers, marking the formal beginning of a scientific discipline that sought to replicate human cognition through technological artifacts. Since then, the concept has evolved significantly, moving from simple task automation to creating sophisticated algorithms for contextual learning and interaction (Haenlein & Kaplan, 2019).

AI can be classified into two broad groups: weak AI (narrow Al) and strong AI (general Al). While the first refers to systems capable of performing specific functions autonomously, such as virtual assistants, facial recognition software, or search engines, the second refers to systems with reasoning and self-awareness capabilities similar to the human brain — a goal not yet fully achieved (Domingos, 2017).

Among the most used technologies are machine learning and deep learning, which consist of methods that allow algorithms to adjust their behavior based on the analysis of large volumes of data, without the need for direct reprogramming, whose models are trained to identify patterns and make predictions with high accuracy (Domingos, 2017). Allied to this, it is worth exposing the aspect that touches computer vision, which allows the automated analysis of images and videos, and natural language processing (NLP), which enables machines to understand, process and respond to commands in human language. Tools such as ChatGPT, assistants such as Siri, and automatic translators are examples of practical applications of NLP (Jurafsky & Martin, 2008).

In the organizational context, AI is being widely used to optimize processes, reduce costs, and increase efficiency, so companies adopt intelligent algorithms to predict market demands, personalize customer service, perform risk analysis, and automate repetitive administrative tasks. Such transformations have direct implications for the structure of work and the dynamics of labor relations (Brynjolfsson & Mcafee, 2014).

Specifically in the workplace, AI has been applied in the recruitment and selection of personnel, with software that analyzes resumes, social media profiles, and interview data to indicate the most suitable candidates. Although efficient, this practice raises concerns about algorithmic impartiality, as algorithms trained with biased data can reproduce historical discriminations (Eubanks, 2018).

Another growing application is in productivity monitoring, with systems that track the pace of employees' work in real time, identifying breaks, response time, and behavior patterns, whose systems promise greater efficiency, but also raise debates about privacy, surveillance, and the right to disconnect (Zuboff, 2021).

In industry and logistics, AI is applied to coordinate production chains, predict machine failures, automatically adjust inventories, and operate autonomous vehicles. Intelligent robots, such as Amazon's, already perform complex tasks with a high degree of autonomy, completely reconfiguring the job profile and requiring new qualifications from workers (Susskind, 2020).

In the legal sector, LA has been used for predictive analysis of judicial decisions, extraction of jurisprudence, automation of petitions, and customer service through chatbots. Tools such as Ross Intelligence, Jurimetria and LegalBot point to a profound change in access to Justice, although still restricted to low-complexity tasks (Catalini; Gans, 2020).

The impact of AI is also felt in the field of healthcare, with assisted diagnosis systems, surgical robots and genomic analysis platforms, but the introduction of AI in medicine nevertheless raises delicate ethical issues, such as professional autonomy, civil liability for algorithmic errors and the protection of sensitive patient data (Topol, 2019).

From the point of view of Law, the challenge is to build regulatory frameworks that keep up with the fast pace of technological innovation, without compromising fundamental rights. The absence of specific legislation in Brazil on AI and labor makes it difficult to provide legal protection for issues such as automated dismissals, algorithm-based promotion criteria, and impacts on workers' mental health (Delgado, 2020).

The legal framework for artificial intelligence in Brazil is still under construction, although the Senate has presented Bill No. 2,338/2023, which aims to establish principles, rights, and duties for the use of AI. Among the project's core principles are non-discrimination, algorithmic transparency, accountability, and human oversight of intelligent systems (Brazil, 2023).

At the international level, the European Union has led the regulation of AI, with the proposal of the Al Act, which classifies AI systems according to the degree of risk and imposes strict requirements for those working in critical sectors. This European model is considered one of the most advanced and has served as an inspiration for other jurisdictions, including Brazil (Europa, 2021).

# AI AS A TOOL FOR MANAGING OCCUPATIONAL RISKS

Occupational risk management is fundamental for the promotion of health and safety at work, as provided for in article 7, item XXII, of the Federal Constitution. In recent years, artificial intelligence (AI) has been consolidated as a strategic ally in this field, allowing the anticipation, assessment, and control of environmental and organizational risks with greater precision and agility (Brazil, 1988).

Through systems based on machine learning, AI can process large volumes of data from sensors, accident histories, medical records, and performance indicators, identifying patterns that escape human analysis, whose analytical capacity has revolutionized the Risk Management Programs (PGR), provided for in NR-1

(Brazil, 2020).

The application of AI in occupational risk management occurs on different fronts, one of the most relevant being the use of intelligent sensors coupled to Personal Protective Equipment (PPEs) and machines, which monitor variables such as temperature, humidity, exposure to toxic gases, and sound pressure in real time. The data collected is analyzed by algorithms that issue automatic risk alerts (Alcantara, 2023).

In addition to environmental monitoring, AI is used in the predictive prevention of accidents, with the analysis of unsafe behaviors recorded by cameras with computer vision. AI systems are able to identify improper movements, incorrect use of PPE, and proximity to danger zones, issuing instant corrective commands (Lee; Yoon, 2021).

These resources contribute to the reduction of subjectivity in risk analyses, providing diagnoses based on quantitative and up-to-date evidence. Unlike traditional methods, based on spot observation and human perception, algorithms work continuously and autonomously, increasing the effectiveness of preventive actions (Liu et al, 2025).

It is also worth highlighting the field of ergonomic evaluation of work, in which AI systems process biomechanical and postural data to identify physical overloads, repetitiveness of movements and time of exposure to harmful postures. This automated diagnosis can be integrated with the PPRA (Environmental Risk Prevention Program) and workplace ergonomics programs (Delgado, 2020).

AI also acts in the management of psychosocial risk through the analysis of internal communication patterns, performance reports, and absenteeism levels: algorithms are trained to detect signs of burnout, chronic stress, and toxic organizational climate, offering managers a predictive tool for interventions before illness (Schiavi, 2022).

However, the use of AI in risk management requires technical and legal responsibility, especially regarding the protection of workers' personal data. The General Data Protection Law (LGPD - Law No. 13,709/2018) imposes clear limits on the collection, processing, and sharing of sensitive data, requiring transparency and legitimate purpose (Brazil, 2018).

Brazilian jurisprudence is still incipient regarding liability for automated decisions in the field of occupational safety, but article 20 of the LGPD provides that the data subject has the right to request the review of decisions made solely on the basis of automated processing, which may include risk alerts or absences resulting from AI (Brazil, 2018). To ensure the ethical use of L in risk management, qualified human intervention in decision-making processes is essential, as proposed by Bill No. 2,338/2023, which deals with the legal framework of LA in Brazil. Human action is a condition for the legitimacy and reliability of intelligent systems, especially in sensitive topics such as occupational health (Brazil, 2023).

The integration between AI and labor compliance is another interesting aspect. Artificial intelligence has been used to perform automated internal audits on compliance with Regulatory Standards, avoiding legal liabilities and promoting safer and more legally adequate work environments (Cabral, 2024).

At the international level, the International Labor Organization (ILO) recognizes the importance of AI in the modernization of occupational safety and health systems, as long as it is accompanied by adequate labor guarantees. In its 2021 report, the ILO argued that digital technologies should be used to protect, not surveil, workers (ILO, 2021).

The responsible adoption of AI in the management of occupational risks requires the technical training of WH teams, the elaboration of ethical protocols for use and the supervision of engineers, occupational physicians and specialized jurists. Only with this tripod - technique, ethics and law - will it be possible to ensure that the benefits of AI are reverted into real protection of the worker's health (Delgado, 2020).

# PREDICTIVE TECHNOLOGIES AND SMART SENSORS

In this regard, it should be noted that predictive technologies consist of systems based on algorithms and data analysis capable of anticipating future events with a high degree of accuracy, helping managers in making preventive decisions. In the workplace, these technologies are applied especially to the prevention of accidents, operational failures and risks to workers' health, promoting a new management paradigm based on anticipation and not just on reaction (Domingos, 2017).

Such technologies use large volumes of data - also called big data - and statistical models, such as neural networks, decision trees, and supervised learning, to identify patterns and infer probabilities. In practice, this allows companies to predict, for example, which workers are most likely to develop repetitive strain injuries or which equipment is most at risk of imminent failure (Brynjolfsson & Mcafee, 2014).

In the context of occupational health and safety (OSH), intelligent sensors represent the main interface between the worker and the LA systems, making devices capable of capturing and transmitting information in real time on environmental (temperature, humidity, noise, toxic gases) and physiological (heart rate, body posture, movement) variables, promoting continuous monitoring of occupational exposure (LEE; Yoon, 2021).

These sensors can be attached to personal protective equipment (PPE), smart clothing, or wearable devices such as bracelets, helmets, and vests. Such resources substantially increase the ability to detect risk situations early, issuing automatic alerts and activating safety protocols when critical conditions are detected (Liu et al, 2025).

The integration between smart sensors and predictive systems forms what is called the "Industrial Internet of Things (IloT), whose integration allows machines, equipment and workers to communicate with each other, creating an intelligent and autonomous ecosystem of accident prevention and operational management (Liu; Guo; Wang, 2025).

One of the main technological innovations in this field is the use of digital dosimeters, which continuously assess exposure to noise, vibrations, and radiation, providing individualized and updated reports on the environmental conditions faced by each worker (Delgado, 2020).

Another relevant application is the use of cameras with computer vision to detect behavioral deviations and unsafe movements in industrial areas. Combined with pattern recognition algorithms, these technologies automatically identify situations such as absence of PPE, displacement in restricted areas, and inadequate postures, enabling immediate interventions (Liu; Guo; Wang, 2025).

In the mining and construction sector, for example, geolocation and acceleration sensors are used to monitor the movement of workers in risk areas, preventing falls, collapses, or collisions with heavy machinery (ILO, 2021).

## AUTOMATION OF HEALTH HAZARDOUS TASKS: ROBOTS, ALGORITHMS, AND MONITORING

The automation of unhealthy tasks is one of the most promising fronts for the application of artificial intelligence (AI) and robotics in the workplace, as it is the strategic use of technologies capable of replacing humans in activities that involve exposure to harmful agents, reducing health risks and preventing occupational illness. This transformation, in addition to being technical, is legal and ethical, requiring a new reading of labor protection standards (Delgado, 2020).

The constitutional basis for this change is supported by article 7, item XXII, of the Federal Constitution of 1988, which guarantees workers the reduction of risks inherent to work, through health, hygiene and safety standards. The replacement of workers by intelligent machines or systems in high-risk tasks is in line with this protective commandment (Brazil, 1988).

On a practical level, collaborative robots (cobots) and autonomous systems have been used to carry out activities in environments with extreme heat, high noise, toxic substances, biological agents and risk of serious accidents. Chemical, metallurgical, mining and hospital industries have adopted these technologies to protect the physical integrity of their professionals (Susskind, 2020).

These robots are equipped with sensors and algorithms that allow them to identify obstacles, recognize objects, adapt their movements, and interact with humans safely. By performing repetitive, heavy or dangerous tasks, they eliminate the worker's direct contact with the unhealthy agent, which, in many cases, extinguishes the factual basis for the payment of the unhealthy bonus (TST, 2023).

The Consolidation of Labor Laws (CLT), in its article 191, provides that the elimination or neutralization of unhealthy conditions can occur through collective protection measures or, in the absence of these, with the effective use of Personal Protective Equipment. The replacement of human activity by robots can be interpreted as a measure of collective protection with a maximum degree of effectiveness (Brasil, 1943).

In addition to physical robots, intelligent algorithms are being used to automate administrative and laboratory processes that previously required handling of contaminating materials. In hospitals, for example, AI systems control stocks of biological waste, perform preliminary patient screenings, and manage disinfection protocols, reducing the exposure of health workers to infectious agents (Topol, 2019).

Robotics also plays an essential role in the food industry. Automated manipulators perform cutting, sealing and thermal processes in cold, humid and polluting environments, previously operated by humans, whose replacement has important labor repercussions, as it requires professional requalification and reorganization of the working day (Haenlein; Kaplan, 2019).

An expanding field is that of remote automation, in which human operators remotely control machines that perform unhealthy tasks: drones, intelligent cranes, autonomous forklifts, and camera inspection systems are examples of technologies that allow the monitoring and control of hostile environments without the physical presence of the worker (Lee; Yoon, 2021).

However, the adoption of robots and algorithms in unhealthy tasks must respect fundamental legal principles, such as the social function of work and the dignity of the human person. The simple replacement of human beings by machines without just transition policies can generate structural unemployment and technological exclusion, deepening existing inequalities (Antunes, 2018).

From a liability perspective, automation does not eliminate the employer's obligation to ensure a safe work environment. Automated systems that have flaws, such as a poorly calibrated algorithm or a faulty robot, can cause damage to the remaining worker or third parties, giving rise to compensation for accident or illness resulting from technological negligence (Garcia, 2021).

It is important to remember that the automation of unhealthy tasks also changes the configuration of typical accidents, since new risks are now related to the failure of control systems, dependence on software, and the cyber vulnerability of machines, requiring new models of prevention, expertise, and regulatory regulation (Europe, 2021). Given this scenario, jurists and labor law operators are challenged to reinterpret classic concepts of labor law in the light of emerging technologies. Unhealthy conditions should not only be combated with additional wages, but above all with technological innovation that eliminates the origin of the risk, in line with the constitutional principles of valuing work and protecting health (Delgado, 2020).

## BENEFITS OF AI IN PREVENTING HARM TO WORKER HEALTH

It is important to note, in this regard, that the advancement of digital technologies has greatly expanded the possibilities of preventive action in workers' health, especially with the incorporation of systems based on artificial intelligence (AI), whose tools have allowed the continuous monitoring of environmental conditions, identification of occupational risks and predictive analysis of occupational illnesses, enhancing individual and collective protection strategies. According to the International Labour Organization (ILO), well-targeted digitalization can transform the occupational environment, making it safer and healthier (ILO, 2025).

AI has proven to be essential for the early detection of patterns that indicate the risk of illness, such as prolonged exposure to toxic substances, repetitive movements, and thermal overload, since sensors coupled to intelligent systems are capable of analyzing the environmental and physiological variables of workers in real time, enabling immediate interventions before damage occurs. This time, as pointed out by the European Agency for Safety and Health at Work (EU-OSHA), these technologies reduce the latency between risk and response, favoring effective preventive actions (EU-OSHA, 2021).

In addition, AI, in the field of occupational health, demonstrates the ability to continuously learn from large volumes of data and, in this way, by processing medical records, accident records, and patterns of behavior at work, algorithms are able to identify complex relationships between variables and propose customized measures for each sector or worker profile. This makes health actions more precise and efficient, as stated by Oliveira et al (2023), when highlighting the importance of AI in optimizing quality of life programs at work.

In addition to primary prevention, AI also contributes to secondary prevention, by identifying subtle symptoms of occupational diseases early and, in this way, applications with machine learning capabilities are able to recognize mood swings, fatigue, or persistent pain from digital interactions, such as keyboard use, voice, or movement patterns. This information is interpreted by intelligent systems that alert health managers about possible problems, allowing the anticipation of diagnoses (ILO, 2025).

In high-risk activities, such as mining, civil construction and transportation, AI has contributed with computer vision systems that detect misconduct or failures in personal protective equipment (PPE), and the monitoring of workers remains possible through cameras coupled to artificial neural networks, issuing alerts when there is non-compliance with safety standards. According to EU-OSHA (2021), these solutions are capable of reducing the incidence of fatal accidents in these sectors.

From the point of view of ergonomics, AI has allowed the development of intelligent wearables capable of adjusting postures, indicating breaks and suggesting adjustments in workstations, whose devices act as personal assistants, teaching workers to preserve their musculoskeletal and mental health during the workday. In this sense, Oliveira et al (2023) observe that the use of artificial intelligence in ergonomics has the potential to minimize leaves due to occupational diseases, especially RSI/WMSD.

The analysis of data from environmental sensors integrated with AI enables a dynamic mapping of risk zones within the work environment, which allows the reorganization of operational flows, avoiding continuous exposure to harmful agents, such as excessive noise, extreme heat or chemicals. The ILO (2025) points out that this data-driven reorganization improves not only the health, but also the productivity and well-being of workers.

AI, likewise, is likely to contribute to the prevention of psychosocial problems by identifying patterns of stress, burnout, and dissatisfaction in the workplace. Therefore, analytical tools that interpret internal communications, work rhythms, and sleep patterns help in the formulation of more effective mental health policies. EU-OSHA (2021) highlights that AI holds promise in creating more humane work environments, as long as it is used ethically and transparently.

It is important to note that the preventive action of AI does not replace human presence, but enhances it and, in this way, by automating repetitive tasks and risk analyses, frees occupational health professionals for more qualified interventions centered on the subjectivity of workers. In this light, Oliveira et al (2023) argue that human-machine integration in the field of occupational health can be an ally of humanization, as long as it is guided by ethical values and social justice.

AI, likewise, supports the rehabilitation and reintegration of workers after sick leaves, which is why clinical decision support algorithms can suggest adaptations of function, rhythm, and workload based on health histories and performance evaluations, reducing the risk of relapse. The ILO (2025) points out that this customization of the return to work is one of the most intriguing advances provided by smart digitalization:

One cannot forget about the possibility of continuous and impartial auditing of working conditions: automatic reports, based on sensors and images, generate evidence that can be used in health surveillance actions, labor inspections and internal audits. This digital traceability strengthens the culture of safety and social responsibility in organizations.

The use of AI in the continuing education of workers also manifests an evolving scenario and, therefore, adaptive platforms offer personalized health and safety content based on individual performance, promoting active and continuous learning. Oliveira et al (2023) highlight that these approaches favor the empowerment of workers, making them active agents in the construction of safer work environments.

From a collective perspective, AI allows cross-referencing intersectoral data to identify social determinants of health at work, such as gender inequality, ethnicity, or religion, whose expanded view contributes to more integrated and equitable public policies, as recommended by the ILO (2025), which advocates the responsible use of technology to combat structural vulnerabilities.

AI-based automation has a positive impact on reducing human exposure to dangerous activities, as robots and autonomous systems, guided by AI, take over unhealthy tasks, such as handling toxic products or activities in confined places, preventing workers from submitting themselves to unnecessary risks.

EU-OSHA (2021) emphasizes that this replacement should be accompanied by reskilling strategies.

Taking into account the above, it is indisputable that AI remains embodied in a strategic tool for governance in occupational health by subsidizing public and private managers with consistent and real-time data. In this vein, interactive panels powered by artificial intelligence help in evidence-based decision-making, optimizing investments in prevention and promoting an organizational culture focused on caring for life, according to Oliveira et al (2023).

# ARTIFICIAL INTELLIGENCE AS DISRUPTIVE INNOVATION

Artificial Intelligence (AI) represents one of the most disruptive innovations of the twenty-first century, not only because of its technical complexity, but mainly because of its ability to redefine social, economic, and legal paradigms, whose disruptive nature lies in the possibility of automating cognitive processes previously exclusive to human beings, such as decision-making, predictive analysis, and adaptive learning. According to Schwab (2016, p.109), "AI is the heart of the Fourth Industrial Revolution, as it goes beyond the physical limits of the machine to act in the sphere of intelligence, perception, and cognition".

In this sense, AI is not just another technology: it is a grassroots transformation that alters the way we produce, relate to, and regulate our social and institutional interactions. As Harari (2018) argues, AI has the potential to change not only what we do, but who we are, as it directly interferes with what once defined human uniqueness.

This disruption is especially noticeable in the field of work. Artificial Intelligence has been changing the forms of production, management and control. The introduction of algorithms for performance analysis, productivity management, and working hours control profoundly changes the nature of the employment relationship. Harari (2018, p.150) warns that "algorithms know more about us than we know ourselves, and this asymmetry of knowledge can generate new forms of domination and surveillance." Thus, the disruption of AI is not limited to the technical level: it reaches the very essence of human relationships mediated by work. According to Schwab (2016), it is necessary to rethink the ethical and legal foundations that sustain labor activity in the face of the rise of intelligent systems

The idea of disruptive innovation also implies resistance. Many of the legal, union, and political institutions still operate on assumptions from the industrial age, which makes it difficult to absorb the impacts of AI. As Souza (2022, p.88) argues, "artificial intelligence imposes an institutional challenge of normative updating and technical training of legal operators, who need to understand the foundations and limits of this technology". This means that the disruption caused by AI cannot be tackled with conservative responses.

It is necessary to develop new theoretical and methodological frameworks that allow dealing with the side effects of intelligent automation.

The disruptive logic of Artificial Intelligence is also manifested in the way it reorganizes power flows in institutional and social structures, so that the ability of intelligent systems to process decisions based on massive data challenges the traditional hierarchical model of authority. As Schwab (2016, p.126) points out, "algorithms are replacing human judgment in areas such as finance, medical diagnostics, and public management, creating new centers of algorithmic decision-making," whose algorithmic centrality requires a new conception of responsibility and accountability, as decisions are no longer made exclusively by identifiable human subjects. For Harari (2018), this shift from authority to algorithms requires a new social contract that includes mechanisms for technical and legal oversight of AI systems.

In this same panorama, it is observed that the disruption of AI also reaches the field of subjectivity and, by being able to learn from human behavior and anticipate actions based on digital profiles, AI transforms individual experience into raw material for automated decisions. This directly impacts the notion of autonomy and free will in labor and consumer relations.

Ferreira (2022, p.65) points out that "the use of behavioral data for decision-making creates asymmetries that affect the self-determination of subjects, making them objects of algorithmic calculation". This depersonalization calls into question the classic guarantees of liberal law and reinforces the need for enhanced protection of personal data and individual freedoms, as Souza (2022) also argues when arguing that the regulation of AI should be guided by the principles of human dignity and distributive equity.

Based on this structural transformation, it is evident that the IL should not be regulated only as a tool, but as a transforming agent of institutional logics and, within this panorama, its disruptive nature lies in the fact that it does not operate in isolation, but integrates interdependent systems that redefine time, space and value in the world of work and justice. Schwab (2016, p.132) observes that "the convergence between AI, biotechnology, and the internet of things creates a new institutional architecture based on speed and connectivity," which requires a cross-cutting and integrated regulatory response, which considers the effects of AI on fundamental rights and on the democratic balance between technology, market, and society. Harari (2018) adds that ignoring this convergence can lead to the obsolescence of institutions and the weakening of public control mechanisms.

In addition, it is important to consider that the disruption promoted by AI imposes new criteria for valuing human work and, by automating cognitive functions, AI redefines what is considered productive work and who are the socially valued subjects. Souza (2022, p.92) argues that "smart technologies can generate a new occupational hierarchy, excluding workers whose skills do not fit the digital model", whose scenario of technological exclusion requires public policies of inclusion and requalification, capable of ensuring that innovation is socially distributed and that the benefits of the LA are not concentrated in a few hands. Ferreira (2022) reinforces that labor law needs to anticipate these changes, recognizing new forms of bonding, competence, and protection in the digital context.

Continuing this reflection, the understanding of AI as a disruptive innovation also requires the recognition of its limits and contradictions and, in this way, intelligent automation can, paradoxically, increase inequalities if applied without ethical criteria and without social compensation mechanisms. Harari (2018, p.157) warns that "algorithms can perpetuate historical injustices by learning from biased data, making automated discrimination even more difficult to detect and correct."

This reinforces the need for the development of the LA to be accompanied by clear normative principles, such as transparency, auditability and social control, arguing Schwab (2016) that emerging technologies must be regulated by a new model of collaborative governance, capable of combining innovation with equity and social justice.

In this context, it is essential that regulatory frameworks keep up with the speed of innovation, promoting not only the adaptation of existing standards, but the creation of new legal devices, capable of responding to the unprecedented challenges posed by AI. Souza (2022, p.96) proposes the construction of a digital labor law that considers the new formats of bonding, remuneration, control, and surveillance. This new right should not only be reactive, but guided by the promotional function of the State, ensuring conditions for the law to be an ally in the promotion of social justice. Harari (2018) complements this view by stating that, in an algorithmic world, the role of the legislator is not only to protect the past, but to imagine and institute fairer and more balanced futures.

# IMPACTS OF ARTIFICIAL INTELLIGENCE ON BRAZILIAN LABOR JUSTICE

## THE INCORPORATION OF ARTIFICIAL INTELLIGENCE IN THE LABOR COURTS

It is important to note, in this regard, that LA has been progressively used in occupational safety management systems, especially in the sectors most exposed to unhealthy conditions. In manufacturing units and construction sites, for example, smart sensors and wearable devices are used to monitor noise, heat, toxic gases, and vibrations in real time.

Such devices, integrated with AI platforms, issue automatic alerts and trigger evacuation protocols, which contributes to the reduction of accidents and continuous exposure to harmful agents (Souza, 2022, p.80). In this regard, Schwab (2016) highlights that intelligent automation not only improves productivity, but redefines the centrality of the worker in the architecture of the production process. This reconfiguration, however, imposes new challenges on labor legislation: unhealthiness, traditionally measured through punctual expertise based on momentary evaluations, must be rethought in light of the continuous data collection promoted by AI.

These data offer a more accurate and dynamic view of the real conditions of the work environment and, according to Pagnanelli and Ravasio (2020, p.53), "the use of artificial intelligence makes it possible to build risk maps updated in real time, breaking with the static logic of traditional reports". In this way, there is an expansion of the capacity for prevention and, simultaneously, a reconfiguration of the way in which the proof of unhealthiness is understood.

The incorporation of Artificial Intelligence (AI) into the Labor Courts represents an institutional inflection point, the analysis of which demands the understanding of its operational and symbolic effects. The ability to process large volumes of data quickly, accurately, and with consistent patterns has made AI an indispensable tool for streamlining forensic routines. Ferreira (2022, p.59) observes that "the experience of the Victor system in the STF demonstrates that AI can assist in the screening of cases and in the identification of repetitive demands, optimizing the time of magistrates for decisions of greater complexity".

This redirection of judicial action allows greater attention to the principles of reasonable duration of the process and efficiency provided for in article 5, item LXXVIII, of the Federal Constitution. In Schwab's (2016) terms, the automation of the repetitive functions of the Judiciary does not mean dehumanization, but rather a reorientation of judicial activities towards what is strategic and interpretative.

It is in this context that the Labor Courts become fertile ground for the use of the law in predictive analysis, extraction of jurisprudence standards and identification of procedural risks. Harari (2018, p.158) points out that "AI adapts to any field structured in language and rules, which makes it ideal for legal systems based on legal texts and precedents".

Thus, the digitalization and computerization of the Labor Courts are the starting point for the construction of a smarter judicial ecosystem, in which the focus is on the substantial guarantee of rights and not only on their formalization. According to Souza (2022), this transition requires public investments, technical training, and regulatory security, in order to ensure that the law is used as a means of enforcing the fundamental rights of the worker.

# AI IN THE PRODUCTION OF EVIDENCE AND PREVENTION OF LABOR LITIGATION

The introduction of artificial intelligence (AI) in the production of evidence and in the prevention of labor litigation has caused a significant transformation in the way labor relations are inspected and judicialized. With the use of environmental sensors, wearable devices, and smart cameras, it is possible to carry out digital forensics and remote inspections of work environments with precision, safety, and agility, as well as to assist companies in structuring healthy environments.

Souza (2022, p.108) states that "AI applied to judicial expertise allows for a continuous and objective analysis of working conditions, providing reliable data that strengthens the judge's conviction and reduces the margin of subjectivity in decisions". In addition to increasing the reliability of expert reports, this technology favors the anticipation of preventive measures, avoiding the worsening of unhealthy conditions and, consequently, the filing of labor lawsuits.

This new evidentiary approach gains special relevance in the context of unhealthy environments, in which simple on-site observation is not always enough to identify the risks to which workers are subjected. With AI, it is possible to continuously monitor these spaces, recording variations in temperature, humidity, suspended particles, and noise, among other indicators.

Ferreira (2022, p.85) points out that "intelligent systems allow capturing evidence in real time, with the ability to store and cross-reference data that would be unfeasible to human perception, providing greater technical robustness to judicial demands". In addition to assisting in the determination of responsibilities in lawsuits already in progress, this automated surveillance capacity creates a fertile field for labor compliance actions, encouraging employers to adopt corrective measures before the damage materializes or worsens.

Another aspect that deserves to be highlighted is the impact of the law on the procedural speed of labor lawsuits, since the automation of the collection and analysis of evidence reduces the time needed to complete expert diligences and produce technical reports. The digitalization of work environments and the integration of databases with analytical intelligence enable more agile responses to lawsuits, optimizing the processing of processes.

According to Ferreira (2022, p.88), "the automation of judicial expertise, added to predictive intelligence in the screening of evidence, promotes a new procedural logic based on the efficiency and rationalization of instructive acts". This reality puts on the agenda the need to restructure the legal procedures themselves, in order to incorporate technology without sacrificing the guarantees of the adversarial process, the ample defense and the impartiality of the judge, fundamental pillars of the fair process.

Based on the applications already observed, it is important to highlight that the law also contributes to the reduction of labor litigation by allowing the early detection of irregularities and risks in the workplace. Automated continuous audit systems can identify misconduct, prolonged exposure to harmful agents and operational failures in real time, providing subsidies for preventive management decision-making, helping companies to structure healthy environments.

Souza (2022, p.111) states that "the automation of inspection routines in the field of occupational safety represents a strategic advance, as it anticipates the diagnosis of critical situations, often neglected due to human or operational limitations". This means that the law not only qualifies the fact-finding process in the course of a lawsuit, but also projects itself as a corporate governance tool, with the potential to positively impact labor relations and organizational culture.

## The Transformation of Forensic Evidence Using Digital Data

Initially, it should be noted that the implementation of AI in the Labor Court also has implications for the model of production of evidence, especially in lawsuits involving unhealthiness, dangerousness, and overtime. Monitoring systems based on sensors, wearables and automated time and attendance records can produce data that, processed by algorithms, objectively support the expert action and the conviction of the magistrate.

Ferreira (2022, p.63) states that "digital data can become more accurate, transparent, and less susceptible to manipulation, conferring greater impartiality to the judicial decision". According to Schwab (2016), the validity of this evidence depends on the transparency of the algorithms, the traceability of the data, and the existence of protocols that ensure the contradictory and the full defense.

In this way, AI does not replace the judge, but redefines the technical bases on which he forms his conviction.

It is relevant to clarify that expert evidence plays a relevant role in the scope of the labor process, especially in claims involving unhealthiness, dangerousness, occupational accidents and occupational diseases. In this scenario, artificial intelligence (AI) has promoted a paradigmatic shift in the way forensics are conducted, documented, and analyzed. The insertion of digital data from smart devices and environmental sensors has given greater precision to the technical analyses carried out by judicial experts, making expert evidence more objective and less subject to subjective controversy (Souza, 2024).

The use of wearable technologies, which monitor heart rate, body movement and exposure to risk agents has become a robust source of digital evidence in forensic investigations, whose data, when processed with the help of the LA, allow detailed reconstructions of the work routine and exposure to harmful conditions. According to Lopes and Pivatto (2023), the replacement of exclusively testimonial narratives with digital records contributes to the strengthening of the principle of real truth, widely enshrined in Labor Law.

By interpreting large volumes of data (big data), AI allows forensics to move from being just a static report based on point observation to a continuous and dynamic process, which is particularly important in cases where health damage results from cumulative and prolonged exposure to risk factors. which was previously difficult to demonstrate. As Moreira and Fernandes (2020) teach, AI enables the materialization of a new type of technical evidence, built based on time series and behavioral patterns.

Allied to this, one cannot fail to mention the use of AI for the automated analysis of images and videos captured in work environments and, in this way, computer vision software can identify risky behaviors, failures in the use of PPE and ergonomic deviations with high accuracy. These records are used in technical expertise as visual evidence, adding probative value to the judicial process. In this sense, Lopes and Pivatto (2023) highlight that, by replacing subjective inferences with objective metrics, AI contributes to the scientific valuation of expert evidence.

The reliability of evidence is also increased with the use of blockchain in the chain of custody of forensic data, since the technology ensures that the data extracted from sensors and devices is not tampered with, giving authenticity to digital evidence. The Judiciary, by recognizing the validity of this evidence with technical support, strengthens the legal certainty of decisions in labor lawsuits.

Moreira and Fernandes (2020) explain that digital traceability is a watershed in the credibility of judicial expertise.

In the context of the Labor Courts, AI also has the potential to assist the experts themselves in the preparation of technical reports and, therefore, intelligent systems offer decision support, indicating applicable technical standards, suggesting legal parameters, and comparing similar cases. This not only speeds up the issuance of reports, but also reduces disparities between technical conclusions in similar situations. In the terms of Souza (2024), this standardization of expert action strengthens the principle of equality between the parties.

It is worth remembering that the insertion of digital data in labor proceedings allows objective evidence to replace the requirement of proof by witnesses, often inhibited or absent. By democratizing access to technical evidence, the law contributes to the effectiveness of the principle of protection, the basis of Labor Law, reinforcing Lopes and Pivatto (2023) that this change promotes greater equity in the judicial process.

In addition, it should be noted that the L has allowed the creation of predictive expert models based on databases fed by previous actions, which are capable of indicating, with a high accuracy rate, the probable occupational origin of a disease, the relationship between tasks and pathologies and even the future risks for entire categories of workers. According to Lopes and Pivatto (2023), this approach transforms expert evidence from a retrospective instrument into a structural prevention tool.

The integration between experts, judges and technical assistants has been improved with intelligent digital platforms that organize and cross-reference expert data, facilitating technical dialogue and critical evaluation of reports. Within this panorama, Moreira and Fernandes (2020) emphasize that AI favors transparency and qualified contestation of technical evidence, breaking with the logic of an "unquestionable" report, which so often undermines the broad defense.

The evolution of expert evidence with the use of digital data and AI is, in the same way, impacting the processing time of cases, taking into account the fact that the automation of technical steps, such as data collection and formatting of reports, significantly reduces the response time of the judicial system. This has direct repercussions on the effectiveness of the judicial provision and on the right to a reasonable duration of the process, as provided for in article 5, item LXXVIII, of the Federal Constitution (Brasil, 1988).

There are also gains when the subject deals with the standardization of reports, with regard to the standardization of jurisprudence and, in this way, AI models that extract recurring elements from reports and decisions allow the identification of predominant legal and technical theses, providing greater stability and predictability to decisions. Souza (2024) argues that this homogenization is essential to ensure legal certainty in the digital age.

# AI AS SUPPORT IN THE INSTRUCTION AND JUDGMENT OF LABOR LAWSUITS

It is interesting to explain, in this regard, that AI tools are already used for the automatic analysis of procedural documents, the recognition of decisional patterns and the organization of evidence, making judicial acts faster and more efficient. As Machado and Colombo (2021) observe, AI does not replace the judge, but acts as an instrument of rational support, expanding the cognitive capacity of the judge in the face of the complexity of litigation.

In the instruction phase, natural language processing (NLP)-based algorithms have been used to automatically identify the controversial points in the initial petitions and defenses, which allows the judge to direct the collection of evidence more precisely, avoiding unnecessary delays. According to Ramos (2022), this functionality of AI contributes to a more objective instruction and to the concentration of instructive acts on topics effectively relevant to the outcome of the case.

In the same way, it is possible to highlight the analysis of documents attached to the process, such as contracts, time records, reports and pay slips, whereby, through automated reading systems, relevant information is extracted, inconsistencies are identified and data is cross-referenced with external databases, such as e-Social and CNIS. This analytical capacity favors the discovery of the real truth and strengthens the search for fair decisions, as highlighted by Machado and Colombo (2021), when they emphasize that the labor judge must be a technician with social sensitivity, but also with scientific support.

Allied to this, the organization and classification of the body of evidence is highlighted, since intelligent systems can suggest the pertinence or irrelevance of certain evidence based on the prevailing case law and the elements presented by the parties. This screening, although it does not replace the judicial decision, helps to rationalize the evidentiary analysis and, according to Souza (2024), AI can work as a kind of "digital clerk, freeing the magistrate from mechanical tasks so that he can focus on evaluative and interpretative aspects of the case.

At the time of the trial, the AI can present automatic summaries of the records, indicating analogous precedents and even prepare drafts of decisions based on previous judgments of the magistrate himself or majority jurisprudence and, although the final decision must remain under human control, this partial automation contributes to the standardization of understandings and the reduction of contradictory decisions. In this approach, Ramos (2022) states that the conscious use of AI can balance the tension between speed and legal certainty.

Predictive systems have also been gaining ground in the field of Labor Courts and, in this vein, based on machine learning algorithms, it is possible to estimate the probability of success of certain legal theses, based on previous decisions and variables of the specific case. This tool has served not only judges, but also parties, allowing the redirection of strategies and the self-resolution of conflicts. In this sense, Machado and Colombo (2021) observe that, although they are not infallible, predictive models favor the intelligent management of the judicial process.

In addition, judges can count on interactive dashboards powered by AI that facilitate the visualization of statistical data of the process and the jurisdictional unit, whose interfaces contribute to the planning of the agenda, the monitoring of goals and the control of productivity, optimizing the magistrate's time. According to Souza (2024), the rational use of data in judicial decision-making is an irreversible path to the modernization of the Judiciary.

AI, in the same way, has an impact on the promotion of equal treatment between the parties, because, by assisting the judge in identifying unconscious patterns and biases, intelligent systems collaborate for the impartiality of decisions. Ramos (2022) highlights that technology, if well applied, can be an ally in the practical realization of the principle of isonomy.

# PROCEDURAL EFFICIENCY AND REDUCTION OF LITIGATION

Regarding procedural efficiency, there is initially talk of the automation of repetitive tasks, such as the screening of actions, the grouping of similar demands, and the filling out of ordinary orders, whose acts, through the help of artificial intelligence, free magistrates and civil servants for activities of greater legal density, as observed by Souza (2021), when highlighting the role of AI in overcoming excessive formalism in the process.

In practice, this rationalization has a direct impact on the reduction of litigation, especially in mass actions, in which the automated identification of cases that deal with the same matter, through textual detection algorithms, allows for rapid referral to specialized panels or joint judgment, avoiding conflicting decisions. Souza (2021) argues that this mechanism acts as an antidote to lottery jurisprudence and reinforces the integrative function of Justice.

In addition, AI contributes to the stimulation of self-settlement, by offering parties objective prognoses about the chances of success of their claims based on the predictive analysis of previous decisions, so that this resource favors early settlements, reduces unnecessary judicialization, and strengthens the culture of consensual conflict resolution. As Toledo and Pessoa (2023) point out, technology can be a catalyst for a more dialogical justice, as long as it is mediated with transparency and respect for the autonomy of the parties.

In addition, it is clear that the law can be used for the purpose of improving public policies for access to justice, because, by processing data on demand flows and profiles of litigants, the Judiciary can identify systemic bottlenecks and promote proactive actions to prevent litigation, such as joint efforts, educational campaigns or restructuring of specialized courts. In this context, Santos (2025) argues that an efficient Judiciary is not only the one that judges well, but the one that judges less out of structural necessity.

AI, likewise, acts in the automation of ordinary procedural acts, such as subpoenas, filings, and deadline control, which reduces material errors and increases the productivity of servers. As a result, deadlines are better met, procedural congestion decreases, and the image of Justice as a slow and ineffective system begins to be reversed. Souza (2021) points out that the modern work process must combine speed with depth, and AI makes this combination viable.

It is important to highlight that the efficiency promoted by the AI is not merely quantitative, taking into account the fact that the use of analytical dashboards, management reports and automated mappings allows the courts to identify jurisprudential trends, productivity bottlenecks and sectors with a high rate of judicialization, enabling a strategic management of the Judiciary. Toledo and Pessoa (2023) highlight that this dimension of AI projects a Judiciary more responsive to social demands.

With regard to the requalification of the judge's time, it can be noted that, when released from operational tasks, the magistrate has more time for legal reflection, critical analysis of the concrete case and qualified reasoning of decisions. This contributes to the quality of the judicial service and reduces the number of appeals arising from fragile sentences. In this way, Santos (2025) argues that technology should be an instrument of intellectual liberation for the magistrate.

With the integration between AI systems and public databases, it is possible to detect procedural fraud, bad faith litigation, and strategic abusive use of the judicial system, which curbs harmful practices and preserves the resources of the Judiciary for legitimate litigation. Souza (2021) states that, by combating the distorted use of justice, AI contributes to restoring the credibility and public function of the process.

The standardization of judicial routines through the law has the power to favor alignment with the principles of efficiency and reasonable duration of the process, provided for in article 5, item LXXVIII, of the Federal Constitution, because, by reducing the processing time without compromising the quality of the jurisdictional provision, the Judiciary begins to fulfill its constitutional functions more rigorously. To Toledo and Pessoa (2023), technology should be an instrument for the realization of fundamental rights, and not for their postponement.

As for the prevention of repeated judicializations due to administrative failures, it is relevant to point out that, when processing information from public agencies and employers, intelligent systems can indicate legal non-conformities even before they turn into litigation. In view of this, Santos (2025) observes that the preventive function of the Judiciary will be increasingly valued, and the law will be conceived as an essential tool in this new institutional design.

Procedural efficiency, likewise, is manifested in the reduction of operating costs, since, with the reduction of the manual workload, the Judiciary can redirect resources to sensitive areas, such as mediation, expertise, and digital inclusion.

This reorganization allows the system to become more accessible, especially for low-income workers who face economic or geographic obstacles to accessing justice. Within this focus, Toledo and Pessoa (2023) emphasize that efficient justice is also inclusive justice.

In this context, the efficiency promoted by AI should be understood as a substantive efficiency, which preserves the constitutional values of the process, while ensuring quality, speed, and material justice. Santos (2025) points out that technology is only justified in the Labor Courts if it contributes to the realization of fundamental social rights, the ultimate purpose of this branch of the Judiciary.

# ETHICAL AND LEGAL RISKS IF AI IN LABOR JUSTICE

It is important to note, from the outset, that although AI tools have the potential to streamline processes and improve judicial efficiency, their use raises concerns about impartiality, transparency, and data protection. As Peck (2021) points out, technological development must be closely linked to regulatory frameworks that guarantee the observance of fundamental rights

In this step, decisions based on AI are generated by machine learning models that do not offer clear explanations of their judgment criteria. This circumstance, known as the "algorithmic black box", affects the principle of motivation of judicial decisions. In this sense, Doneda (2019) warns that the lack of algorithmic transparency can compromise the very legitimacy of the jurisdiction.

In addition, the introduction of AI in the Labor Courts raises concerns about the depersonalization of justice, in which the jurisdictional activity involves contextual analysis, interpretation of the concrete case and sensitivity to the parties involved, aspects that cannot always be reduced to statistical standards. Peck (2021) highlights that the use of automated systems must respect the limits of human action, otherwise it will dehumanize the jurisdictional provision.

Furthermore, one cannot forget about the reproduction of discriminatory biases and, in this way, the algorithms are trained based on large volumes of historical data that, in turn, reflect the already existing social and economic asymmetries.

As Doneda (2019) warns, AI can internalize structural biases present in training data, generating biased and discriminatory decisions in the work environment.

This scenario is particularly delicate in the Labor Courts, whose performance is guided by the search for equity, and it is certain that the eventual adoption of AI systems that reproduce discriminatory patterns may compromise the social function of the labor jurisdiction, which is why Peck (2021) warns, in this vein, about the need for constant audits of the algorithms to prevent these distortions.

From a legal point of view, there is also the discussion that deals with accountability for decisions made by AI systems, asking, from the outset: who would be responsible for any errors or injustices promoted by automated decisions? According to Doneda (2019), the Brazilian legal system still does not have a clear regime for imputing liability to algorithmic agents, which can make it difficult to repair damages caused by these tools.

Such an issue may violate the right to due process of law and to the right to be heard, since the aggrieved party may have difficulties in challenging a decision whose basis is incomprehensible. In this sense, Peck (2021) observes that, in order to ensure a broad defense, it is necessary that the functioning of the algorithms be understandable and auditable by experts and lawyers.

Furthermore, one cannot forget the protection of personal data in the use of AI, Taking into account the fact that, within the scope of the Labor Courts, there is sensitive personal and professional information in dispute, such as medical records, salary records, and performance data, Doneda (2019) highlights that the automated processing of this data must respect the principles of the General Law for the Protection of Personal Data (LGPD), in particular the purpose, adequacy and necessity.

Therefore, the adoption of artificial intelligence (AI) in the Brazilian Judiciary raises relevant ethical and legal questions, especially with regard to the protection of personal data, the transparency of the algorithms used, and the risk of dehumanization of judicial decisions. With the General Law for the Protection of Personal Data (Law No. 13,709/2018) in force, any automated processing of information in the judicial sphere must respect principles such as purpose, necessity, security, and accountability.

According to Ferreira (2022, p.92), "data protection in the use of AI in the Judiciary is not just a technical requirement, but an ethical and constitutional imperative that ensures the right to intimacy and informational self-determination". This implies that the collection, storage and analysis of judicial and procedural data by intelligent systems must be subject to strict controls, under penalty of violation of the fundamental rights of those under jurisdiction.

Thus, it is essential to advance the discussion on algorithmic transparency, understood as the right to know which parameters are being considered by an AI system when processing data and suggesting legal solutions The absence of clear explanations about the inner workings of algorithms can generate legal uncertainty and undermine public confidence in automated decisions.

Souza (2022, p.117) warns that "the opacity of algorithms compromises the legitimacy of the judicial process, especially when the affected party does not understand the criteria used for decision-making". Thus, transparency must be accompanied by auditability and external validation mechanisms, ensuring that the systems act with impartiality, predictability, and adherence to the constitutional principles of adversarial and full defense.

In addition to the LGPD, the principle of informational self-determination must be observed, which means ensuring that individuals have control over how their data is used by automated judicial systems. In this light, Peck (2021) argues that the autonomy of the data subject must be respected even in contexts in which the data subject is used for public purposes, as is the case of the Judiciary.

The absence of express consent or clear information about the use of AI can compromise the trust of the parties in the process and, therefore, the legitimacy of the use of technology in Justice therefore involves the transparency and governance of the data used in automated decision systems. In this area, Doneda (2019) reinforces that opacity in data processing can be interpreted as an affront to the principle of good faith.

Still on ethical risks, it is worth exposing the erosion of public trust in judicial institutions, because if the parties perceive that decisions are being made by insensitive "machines" and with obscure criteria, the very symbolic value of Justice can be compromised. Peck (2021) points out that the credibility of the Judiciary depends on citizens' perception of justice and legitimacy.

There is, likewise, the risk that the use of AI is motivated exclusively by criteria of managerial efficiency to the detriment of the quality and justice of decisions, and it is certain that the Labor Courts, due to their protective nature, cannot be reduced to productivity goals. Doneda (2019) warns that quantitative indicators should not replace qualitative criteria in the evaluation of judicial performance.

From an institutional point of view, there is a risk that the law will be used as an instrument for the forced standardization of decisions, ignoring the particularities of each process, whose standardization, if applied indiscriminately, can lead to automated justice that contradicts the principles of individualization and proportionality. Doneda (2019) explains, in this regard, that the standardization of decisions, although efficient, cannot be taken as an absolute value.

The use of AI requires the definition of objective criteria for its implementation, in order to avoid arbitrariness and violations of fundamental rights. Peck (2021) argues that it is essential to establish an ethical-normative framework for the responsible use of artificial intelligence in the Judiciary, with continuous oversight and participation of civil society.

# THE ROLE OF THE JUDICIARY IN THE FACE OF THE AUTOMATION OF THE WORK ENVIRONMENT

In this regard, it is appropriate to delimit that the growing automation of the labor environment imposes new challenges and responsibilities on the labor judiciary regarding the protection of fundamental rights, so that the use of technologies such as artificial intelligence, robotics, and algorithms in the production process transforms the forms of hiring, control, and evaluation of human labor. For Cabral et al. (2024), this scenario requires vigilant and critical action by the Judiciary so that the dignity of the worker is not subjugated to economic interests.

The Judiciary cannot omit itself in the face of the structural changes in the world of work promoted by automation, and its constitutional function is to proceed with the interpretation and application of Labor Law in order to safeguard its social and protective function. Gusmão (2022) points out that labor justice must take an active position in the face of new forms of labor exploitation, which often mask employment relationships under the cloak of technology.

The replacement of workers by automated systems directly impacts the principle of social valorization of work and, in many cases, companies use digital tools to intensify the demand for productivity and exercise permanent control over employee performance. Cabral et al. (2024) warn of the risk of these practices configuring a new form of precariousness under the appearance of innovation.

In addition to the impact on formal jobs, automation, in the same way, is capable of affecting the quality of the employment relationship: digital platforms have promoted the so-called "uberization" of labor relations, with exhausting working hours, absence of social protection and absence of union representation. Gusmão (2022) argues that the Judiciary should recognize these phenomena as forms of fraud to labor legislation and apply the principle of the primacy of reality.

In this sense, the role of the Judiciary is indispensable to prevent technology from being used as an instrument for the suppression of rights and, therefore, judicial decisions need to reflect the constitutional commitment to social justice, as recommended by article 7 of the Federal Constitution. Cabral et al. (2024) emphasize that the Judiciary must act as a counterweight to the economic power of technological corporations.

In this scenario, it is essential that the Judiciary develops sensitivity to perceive the new forms of subordination camouflaged in atypical contracts mediated by algorithms, because, for example, the control exercised by applications often equals or exceeds the directive power of the traditional employer. Gusmao (2022) states that the recognition of the employment relationship in these situations is an ethical and legal requirement.

Another relevant aspect is the need to reinterpret labor standards in the light of technological transformations, and it is not a matter of making rights more flexible, but of adapting them to ensure their effectiveness in the face of new forms of work organization. Cabral et al. (2024) highlight that Labor Law must maintain its counter-majoritarian character.

It cannot be left out that the Judiciary must take a critical position regarding the hegemonic narrative that automation is a neutral and inevitable phenomenon, considering that, in practice, the adoption of technologies in the workplace is the result of political and economic choices. Gusmao (2022) points out that judicial neutrality in the face of these choices can legitimize practices that are harmful to workers.

The use of software for performance evaluation, productivity control, and personnel management can violate the worker's intimacy and dignity, which is why labor jurisprudence needs to establish clear limits to the use of these tools, especially when they involve constant surveillance or processing of sensitive data. Cabral et al. (2024) warn that the right to disconnect and privacy must be protected even in highly automated environments.

In addition, the Judiciary has a fundamental role in preserving the principle of non-discrimination, which can be compromised by automated decisions and, therefore, algorithms used in recruitment and selection, for example, can reproduce structural prejudices. Gusmão (2022) argues that it is up to the Judiciary to ensure that the use of these technologies is in accordance with human rights and the principles of decent work.

There are still impacts on automation in relation to forms of collective representation and union bargaining, whose fragmentation, promoted by digital platforms, hinders the organization of workers, requiring an institutional response that favors social dialogue. Gusmao (2022) proposes that the Judiciary contribute to strengthening the role of unions in the face of new productive arrangements mediated by technology.

The pedagogical role of the Judiciary is manifested in the construction of precedents that discourage abusive practices and, in this way, jurisprudence should serve as a guideline to guide business conduct and encourage the ethical use of technologies at work. Gusmao (2022) argues that judicial decisions that are grounded and committed to social rights have a transformative function in the social fabric.

Automation has implications for the concept of working time, working hours, and rest: digital tools make the separation between professional and personal life tenuous, and it is up to the Judiciary to reinterpret these institutes to ensure that workers' health is not sacrificed in the name of efficiency, which is why Cabral et al. (2024) propose a humanistic approach to working time in the digital age.

## THE ROLE OF LABOR LAW IN THE FACE OF AUTOMATION

The advancement of digital technologies and the massive introduction of artificial intelligence (AI) in work environments have required a profound reconfiguration of Labor Law. Historically conceived to balance the relationship between capital and labor in an analog scenario, the labor legal system today faces the challenge of preserving the fundamental principles of worker protection in the face of increasing automation. According to Ferreira (2022, p.74), "technology cannot be used as a justification for the precariousness of the social guarantees conquered, and the Law must remain as an instrument to contain structural inequalities". This position reinforces the centrality of the principle of human dignity in the labor context, whose effectiveness depends on the normative capacity to keep up with technological transformations without giving up minimum protection and equity in labor relations.

From this finding, it becomes evident that normative updating is an essential condition for the effectiveness of social protection in an increasingly automated economy. The legal system needs to dialogue with the new work formats that have emerged from automation, such as AI-assisted remote work, the operation of autonomous systems, and algorithmic task management. Souza (2022, p.102) observes that "labor standards must adapt to the new technological context". In this sense, the regulation of AI-mediated work must consider, for example, the definition of responsibility in the event of operational failures, the protection of sensitive workers' data, and the guarantee of transparency in automated decisions, especially those related to hiring, remuneration, and dismissal of personnel.

The need to modernize labor legislation is also imposed in the face of the transformations in the forms of subordination and control promoted by digital platforms and AI systems. The traditional concept of legal subordination, which underlies a large part of CLT contracts, loses its effectiveness when labor control is exercised through algorithms and automated metrics. Ferreira (2022, p.76) states that "artificial intelligence challenges the classic categories of Labor Law, requiring a rereading of the criteria of subordination, habituality, and onerousness in the light of algorithmic logic". This scenario requires, therefore, an interpretative approach that expands the scope of existing norms and, at the same time, encourages the production of legislation capable of recognizing and disciplining the new forms of control and organization of work.

## THE EXPERIENCE OF THE VICTOR SYSTEM IN THE SUPREME COURT

The development of the Victor system by the Federal Supreme Court (STF) represents one of the most emblematic initiatives in the application of artificial intelligence (AI) in the Brazilian Judiciary. Created with the aim of assisting in the screening and analysis of cases with general repercussion, the system uses algorithms trained on large databases to identify, with high accuracy, the predominant legal issues in extraordinary appeals. Ferreira (2022, p.63) clarifies that *Victor was conceived to optimize the procedural flow of the STF, prioritizing efficiency without compromising decisional coherence and legal certainty". This initiative reflects an institutional attempt to address the procedural accumulation through technological solutions, reaffirming the importance of innovation as a public management tool in contemporary times.

From this perspective, it is possible to observe that the implementation of the Victor system in the STF inaugurates a new phase in the relationship between Law and technology, marked by the integration of AI tools in the judicial decision-making process. The system is capable of reading thousands of petitions in a reduced time, classifying them by subject and identifying repetitive demands, which contributes significantly to the relief of the Court. According to Ferreira (2022, p.64), "by employing machine learning techniques, Victor reduces the dependence on human analysis, without, however, eliminating the role of the judge in the decisive moment of the controversy". This demonstrates that, even in the face of a high degree of automation, judicial activity continues to require ethical and legal criteria that only human reason can ensure, reinforcing the idea that AI should act as a support, and not as a substitute, for the magistrate.

Despite the advances obtained with the implementation of the Victor system, the technical and institutional limitations that accompany the introduction of artificial intelligence in the judicial sphere cannot be neglected. One of the main challenges refers to the opacity of algorithms, whose operating logic is not always understandable by users of the legal system, which can compromise the transparency and legitimacy of decisions. Ferreira (2022, p.66) recognizes that "the algorithmic black box constitutes a relevant obstacle to the social and legal control of automated tools, requiring the construction of auditing and explainability mechanisms". In addition, there is a need to ensure that algorithms are trained with quality data, free of historical biases that may reproduce structural inequalities in the judgment of similar cases. This reinforces the thesis that AI must be accompanied by clear governance parameters, constant human supervision and periodic review of its results.

In this context, one of the aspects that deserves to be highlighted is the contribution of the Victor system to the standardization of jurisprudence and the rationalization of the analysis of precedents in the STF. AI, by identifying recurring patterns and already consolidated decisions, helps ministers and advisors to maintain coherence and predictability in judgments, essential elements for legal certainty. Ferreira (2022, p.67) emphasizes that "the ability to organize and filter large volumes of legal information allows the Victor system to indicate relevant precedents, saving time and favoring decisions more in line with the dominant jurisprudence". This resource has the potential to improve institutional efficiency without compromising the constitutional foundations of due process, since the final decision remains in the hands of the magistrate. In this way, AI proves to be an ally in the consolidation of a more accessible, faster, and reliable judicial system.

# PRECEDENT 448, ITEM II, OF THE SUPERIOR LABOR COURT

## CONTENT PROVIDED FOR IN THE PRECEDENT UNDERSTANDING

Precedent 448, item II, of the Superior Labor Court, provides that:

UNHEALTHY ACTIVITY. CHARACTERIZATION. PROVISION IN REGULATORY NORM NO. 15 OF MINISTRY OF LABOR ORDINANCE NO. 3,214/78. SANITARY FACILITIES.

II - The cleaning of sanitary facilities for public or collective use of large circulation, and the respective garbage collection, as it is not equivalent to cleaning in homes and offices, gives rise to the payment of an additional amount of unhealthiness to the maximum degree, in accordance with the provisions of Annex 14 of NR-15 of MTE Ordinance No. 3,214/78 regarding the collection and industrialization of urban garbage.

According to the collated summary understanding, it is held that the performance of activities performed in bathrooms of high circulation could not be equated to the common cleaning of homes and offices, and should be recognized as unhealthy to the maximum degree, under the terms of Annex 14, of NR-15, of Ordinance No. 3,214/78 of the Ministry of Labor and Employment (MTE), which would imply the payment of the unhealthy bonus in its maximum degree, which, under the terms of labor legislation (article 192 of the CLT), is equivalent to 40% of the current minimum wage.

Precedent 448, item II, of the Superior Labor Court, consolidates a protective understanding regarding the characterization of unhealthy hygiene in sanitary facilities for collective use and large circulation. For Delgado (2020), unhealthy work is a legal institute that aims to protect the health and physical integrity of workers from harmful agents in the work environment. The cleaning of public bathrooms, given their nature and exposure to biological agents, would fit into this protective logic of Labor Law.

This interpretation recognizes the sanitary insalubrity present in the activity of cleaning public bathrooms, understanding that such activity can expose the worker to harmful biological agents, such as viruses, bacteria and human organic waste at high frequency, and that the reality of environments for collective use — such as bus stations, schools, shopping malls, hospitals, among others — would offer risks greater than those found in conventional private or administrative environments.

By determining that the cleaning of public restrooms and the collection of garbage in these areas constitute unhealthy to the maximum degree, the TST recognizes that such activities involve direct contact with human waste, organic waste and potentially pathogenic microorganisms. Barros (2017) argues that, when interpreting labor standards, the actual risk to the worker's health should be considered and not just the formal description of the function or the workplace.

Delgado (2020) argues that Precedent 448/II corrects a historical distortion in which employers unduly equated the cleaning of environments with a large circulation of people — such as bus stations, hospitals, and schools — to domestic or administrative environments, disregarding the high degree of biological risk involved. In this way, consolidated case law advances in the protection of the health of urban cleaning and general service workers.

According to Barros (2017), this summary reaffirms the importance of the qualitative analysis of the environment and the activity performed, and not only its formal framework. By eliminating the analogy between the cleaning of public bathrooms and the cleaning of offices or homes, the TST reinforces the protective nature of Labor Law and, in this way, the Court's jurisprudence consolidated in this precedent understands that the risk to health in these activities is equivalent to that faced by workers involved with the collection and treatment of urban waste, as provided for in Annex 14 of NR-15, which justifies the classification at the maximum degree of unhealthiness.

From the perspective of fundamental rights, Barros (2017) relates the content of the precedent to article 7, item XXII, of the Federal Constitution, which ensures the reduction of risks inherent to work through health, hygiene and safety standards.

Delgado (2020) raises the recognition in the sense that unhealthiness to the maximum degree could not be ruled out by technical reports that disregard the concrete reality of the environment, which is why the judge must, in these cases, evaluate the expert evidence based on criteria of reasonableness and proportionality, especially when there are objective elements that evidence the worker's exposure to health hazardous agents.

Taking into account the above, it is possible to conclude that Precedent 448, item II, of the Superior Labor Court (TST), provides for the characterization of unhealthiness in work activities carried out in environments with sanitary facilities, especially those with collective use and poor hygiene. The precedent understanding establishes that, under these conditions, it is possible to recognize the unhealthiness bonus to the maximum degree, especially when habitual exposure to biological agents is verified.

The application of the precedent does not occur automatically. It is necessary to make a technical finding by means of an expert report prepared by a qualified professional based on the Regulatory Standards of the Ministry of Labor and the recognized technical parameters, in order to recognize or not the unhealthiness. In this sense, the judicial expertise assumes an indispensable role in the assessment of the real environmental conditions, and may even rule out the incidence of the additional if it verifies the absence of exposure to unhealthy agents at harmful levels.

From the point of view of companies, this perspective is relevant since the jurisprudence itself has recognized that, in many cases, the existence of shared bathrooms or locker rooms, by itself, does not constitute an unhealthy environment, especially when there is proof of regular cleaning, provision of adequate Personal Protective Equipment (PPE) and adoption of control measures. Thus, Precedent 448 should be understood as an interpretative guideline subject to the concrete analysis of each situation based on the technical evidence produced in the records.

## PRACTICAL ANALYSIS OF AUTOMATED TOILETS

The technological evolution applied to sanitary facilities in the workplace has provided solutions that directly impact the discussion about unhealthy conditions and, thus, the so-called "automated bathrooms" represent a concrete example of how structural modernization can contribute to minimizing or even eliminating the exposure of workers to unhealthy agents.

Such facilities, usually equipped with flush sensors, automatic faucets, forced ventilation systems and strict hygiene protocols, tend to significantly reduce the biological risk and, in this context, the technical expertise, when analyzing the objective conditions of the site, can conclude that there is no unhealthiness, even if the activity involves collective use of toilets, due to the effective neutralization of risk agents.

For example, it should be noted that, as of November 2024, the population of Belo Horizonte now has five self-cleaning public toilets installed in the central region of the city. The initiative is part of the municipal program "Centro de Todos", coordinated by the City of Belo Horizonte (PBH), which formalized a contract worth R$ 1 million with the company CleanSe, as published in the Official Gazette of the Municipality (DOM) last Friday (18) (Itatiaia, 2024).

The equipment has automated opening, closing and cleaning technology, a stainless steel structure with an anti-vandalism system and guaranteed accessibility for people with disabilities. The design was designed to combine functionality and safety, promoting comfort and dignity in the use of public space. Each self-cleaning public toilet has a monthly cost of R$ 17,500, and the term of the agreement, which began in November 2024, is 12 months from the date of signing, and can be extended for up to five years, according to PBH (Itatiaia, 2024).

CleanSe, winner of the bidding process, already operates similar equipment in cities such as Balneario Camboriu and Sao Jose, in Santa Catarina. The bathrooms follow the model adopted in cities such as Paris, France, with anti-vandalism technology and autonomous cleaning operation. Self-cleaning toilets use national technology and were designed to ensure durability, ease of maintenance and continuous use. The system allows for quick replacement of parts and uninterrupted operation even in the event of breakdowns (Itatiaia, 2024).

Each sanitary unit consists of two individual cabins, both equipped with a toilet, sink, liquid soap dispenser, toilet paper, hand dryer and trash can, with guaranteed daily supply, and all the activation of the devices - such as the release of water, soap and activation of the dryer - is done by means of proximity sensors, which eliminates the need for physical contact and significantly reduces the risk of contamination by microbiological agents. As a means of facilitating use, an audio message guides the user on the correct use of the space (Belo Horizonte City Hall, 2024).

The doors have light signaling to indicate the status of the cabin: "free" (green light), "off" (red light), "occupied" (yellow light) and "cleaning in progress" (blue light). Automatic closing occurs after 10 seconds of inactivity, although the door can also be opened and closed manually as per the user's need. In case of emergency, an internal sensor can be activated, promoting the automatic opening of the door for a period of two minutes (Belo Horizonte City Hall, 2024).

The cleaning process is completely automated and, as soon as the cabin is vacated, sensors detect the absence of human presence and activate the sanitization system. Cleaning is carried out by means of sprinklers (hydraulic showers) installed on the floor, which spray water and disinfectant products, ensuring the asepsis of the environment before the next use (Belo Horizonte City Hall, 2024).

More specifically in Paris, public toilets are fully automated and perform complete sanitization after each use. In this way, as soon as the door is closed, the system comes into action, washing the toilet seat, disinfecting the floor and sterilizing the entire interior of the cabin with jets of water and specific products. The initiative combines technological innovation with the promotion of public health, ensuring high standards of cleanliness even in areas of high circulation, and has served as a reference for several cities around the world (Amorim, 2025).

These sanitary units carry out a self-cleaning cycle between each use, and the light indicators inform the situation of the cabin: "Occupe" signals that it is occupied; "Lavage" indicates that it is in the process of being sanitized - which can be perceived by the characteristic sound similar to that of a dishwasher; "En service" means that the unit is available; and "Hors service" points out that the equipment is out of operation (Secrets of Paris, 2020).

To use it, just press the opening button and the door opens automatically. In order for the door to close and lock automatically, the button with closing arrows must be pressed without the need for manual contact. The door remains locked until the user presses the open button or automatically after 15 minutes – avoiding long stays inside the cab. In the event of a system failure, an emergency red lever can be activated for manual opening (Secrets of Paris, 2020).

The interior is equipped with a sink, mirror, liquid soap dispenser, toilet paper (subject to replacement), hooks for personal belongings and a dual flush system - with buttons for triggering light or strong flow, and the flushes are only effectively triggered after the user has left, as part of the automated cleaning cycle. At the end of use, when leaving the cabin, the door closes automatically and the system starts a cleaning process that lasts about 15 seconds. The procedure makes it essential to wait for the cycle to finish before a new use, as entering immediately after the previous user can result in exposure to water from the washing process (Secrets of Paris, 2020).

It is important to emphasize that the labor courts, although they adopt Precedent 448 as a jurisprudential guideline, have considered expert evidence as decisive in the formation of judicial conviction, and in several lawsuits, the report prepared by a qualified professional demonstrated that the presence of automated bathrooms, combined with effective cleaning and maintenance routines, removes the characterization of unhealthiness, even in activities that would previously be considered presumed risk.

From the employer's point of view, such investments in infrastructure and biosafety protocols not only contribute to the protection of workers' health, but also reinforce the technical defense in any lawsuit. Thus, the practical analysis of these environments reinforces that the discussion about unhealthiness cannot be generic or presumed, requiring a case-by-case, technical and contextualized evaluation.

# AI CONTRIBUTIONS: AUTOMATED TOILETS

Taking into account the above, it is observed that the incorporation of artificial intelligence (AI) in public sanitary facilities represents a technological innovation that directly contributes to the elimination or significant mitigation of occupational risks provided for in Precedent 448, item II, of the Superior Labor Court (TST). The aforementioned precedent recognizes as unhealthy to the maximum degree the hygiene of public bathrooms or for collective use of large circulation, due to the direct exposure of workers to potentially pathogenic biological agents, such as viruses, bacteria and human organic waste, as provided for in Annex 14 of NR-15 of Ordinance No. 3,214/78 of the Ministry of Labor and Employment.

In this context, the application of AI to self-cleaning and sanitary automation systems has transformative potential in facing the unhealthy conditions traditionally associated with this activity, since, through intelligent sensors, automated actuators, and control algorithms, self-cleaning toilets are able to perform complex cleaning procedures without the need for direct human intervention. This means that AI can operate as a technical element for the elimination of the unhealthy agent - a measure provided for as a priority in the regulatory standards before the granting of the unhealthy bonus (NR-15, item 15.4.1).

The use of AI in this equipment makes it possible to identify usage patterns, automatically trigger cleaning cycles, and precisely control the dosage of disinfectant products, ensuring high standards of asepsis with resource savings and health safety. In addition, systems with self-learning capabilities can adjust the frequency and intensity of cleaning according to peak usage times and operation history, optimizing operation in real time.

This intelligence embedded in the equipment is also capable of providing greater traceability of cleaning actions, generating automatic reports of use and hygiene, which can be accessed by public managers for the purposes of inspection, auditing and continuous improvement of the service, whose traceability responds directly to the demand for transparency and sanitary control in public spaces, while also preserving workers from unhealthy and repetitive tasks, such as manually cleaning toilets, floors, and contaminated areas.

In addition, by reducing the need for labor in tasks of high biological risk, AI contributes to the reconfiguration of working conditions in the urban cleaning sector, shifting the focus from human action to supervision, technical maintenance, and operational control functions. This displacement values intellectual and technical work and promotes better occupational health conditions, in line with the constitutional principles of human dignity and the valorization of work, provided for in arts. 1, III, and 7, XXII, of the Federal Constitution.

Artificial intelligence, likewise, has the ability to collaborate with the promotion of universal accessibility, by allowing people with disabilities to interact with sanitary systems without the need for physical contact with surfaces, minimizing architectural and sanitary barriers. Through the use of proximity sensors, voice commands, and automated light signaling, smart toilets provide inclusion, autonomy, and safety, following the guidelines of the Convention on the Rights of Persons with Disabilities, incorporated into the Brazilian legal system with the status of a constitutional norm (Decree No. 6,949/2009).

Another relevant aspect concerns the role of AI in the preventive management of failures. Systems equipped with artificial intelligence are capable of identifying operating anomalies and automatically triggering corrective or preventive maintenance protocols, whose capacity not only ensures the continuity of public service, but also prevents workers from being exposed to contaminated environments due to equipment failure, reinforcing the principle of preventing damage to health in the workplace.

The application of AI in automated bathrooms is equally relevant from a budgetary and strategic point of view, because, even though the initial implementation costs are higher than those of conventional bathrooms, the gains from the reduction of labor liabilities, savings in inputs, risk mitigation, and enhancement of the institutional image justify the investment from a long-term perspective. as demonstrated by experiences such as that of Paris and, more recently, of Belo Horizonte.

It is worth mentioning that, as emphasized by authors such as Delgado (2020) and Barros (2017), Labor Law must be in constant dialogue with social and technological advances. In this way, the adoption of automated smart toilets exemplifies a concrete practice in which technology can be used to enforce social labor rights, not as a form of indiscriminate replacement of the workforce, but as a tool to promote health, safety and dignity in the exercise of functions that traditionally involve high risk.

In view of the above, it must be considered that the application of technologies based on artificial intelligence (AI) has expanded the possibilities of environmental control and prevention of biological risks in environments such as bathrooms for collective use and, in this way, intelligent systems integrated with the sanitary infrastructure allow, for example, real-time monitoring of the frequency of use, detection of failures in hygiene and automatic activation of cleaning and disinfection procedures.

These advances have been incorporated into architectural projects aimed at occupational safety with a direct impact on discussions about the existence or not of unhealthiness, and, from a technical point of view, the lA allows not only to automate cleaning processes, but also to generate auditable reports and records that can support corporate defense in judicial investigations.

Although Precedent 448 of the TST establishes criteria for the characterization of unhealthiness in toilets for collective use, the existence of technologies such as presence sensors, automated dispensers and ozone or UV-C light disinfection systems can be a decisive element for the expert conclusion due to the absence of risk. It is essential, therefore, to understand that AI, when applied in a planned manner, can be an ally in neutralizing unhealthy agents, as long as its operation is demonstrated by technical documentation, maintenance routines, and validation of effectiveness. In summary, automated toilets using wool, more than representing a technological solution with the potential to safeguard the health of workers, strengthen the company's legal position in labor lawsuits, as long as the technical evidence proves the effective mitigation of risks.

# APPLICATION OF AI IN THE REDUCTION OF HEALTH HAZARDOUS WORK

The replacement of human labor by robots in unhealthy environments represents one of the most promising fronts for the application of artificial intelligence (AI) in the world of work. The automation of dangerous, repetitive tasks or tasks exposed to harmful agents has the potential to drastically reduce the rates of illness and occupational accidents, contributing to the promotion of health and safety at work. Harari (2018, p.157) points out that as robots become smarter and more agile, it will be possible to keep humans away from risky activities, such as mining, handling toxic products, and cleaning up industrial waste*. This possibility, however, requires structural investments and public policies to encourage innovation, so that the gains are not limited to large business conglomerates, but extend to critical and vulnerable sectors of the economy.

Continuing the reflection on the automation of unhealthy environments, it is necessary to consider that robots not only replace labor in risky activities, but also introduce a new paradigm of safe productivity. The use of robotic arms in chemical production lines, for example, avoids human contact with corrosive and volatile substances. Schwab (2016, p.111) argues that cyber-physical systems not only optimize industrial performance, but also redefine the role of the worker, who starts to operate as a supervisor of automated processes*. This indicates a transition from direct physical work to monitoring functions, which requires professional reskilling and institutional adaptations in technical training systems and regulatory standards.

In this scenario, it is observed that the replacement of human labor by machines in risky activities is already a reality in sectors such as mining, in which robots are used to map galleries, extract minerals, and operate in areas at risk of collapse. Ferreira (2022, p.68) points out that the use of autonomous vehicles in underground environments not only reduces accidents but also improves the operational performance of companies, with fewer interruptions and lower costs with sick leaves.

However, Souza (2022) warns that the introduction of technology should not be confused with neutrality: automated systems can reproduce or even aggravate inequalities if they are adopted without social criteria and without just transition programs for replaced workers.

With the advancement of AI-based technologies, collaborative robotics emerges as an effective solution to unhealthy tasks that require precision and safety. These robots, called 'cobots', are programmed to work side-by-side with humans, reducing the time of exposure to risks without necessarily eliminating human intervention.

Schwab (2016, p.119) points out that "collaboration between man and machine opens a new horizon for more ergonomic and less exclusionary work environments, where the focus becomes the physical and mental protection of the worker". However, Harari (2018) warns that this integration must be accompanied by a robust regulatory apparatus, in order to ensure that the boundaries between automation and precariousness are not blurred. This reinforces the role of the State in mediating these technological processes.

Therefore, it is easy to see that artificial intelligence (AI) has been consolidated as a strategic tool in promoting safer work environments, especially due to its ability to identify risk patterns and enable immediate interventions. More specifically, in the context of health hazardous work, AI can act significantly in relation to the prevention of exposure to harmful agents, including in places traditionally considered critical, such as collective sanitary facilities.

However, it should be noted that the simple use of intelligent technologies does not imply, by itself, the recognition or removal of the unhealthy bonus, and it is certain that the evaluation of working conditions remains linked to the performance of judicial technical expertise, which should verify whether, in practice, the systems implemented are effective in neutralizing risks. The expert report, therefore, continues to be the central element in the formation of the conviction of the court.

Experience shows that, in several cases, the expert opinion concludes that there is no unhealthiness, especially when the company presents technical documentation, maintenance reports, cleaning control and evidence of the functionality of intelligent systems. In other cases, even with the presence of technologies, the expert can attest to the existence of unhealthiness, if the procedures are inoperative or insufficient in view of the identified risks.

Therefore, what is observed in practice is that the law contributes to the construction of safer work environments, but its legal impact will depend on concrete evidence and the individualized analysis of each situation. In this scenario, the employer's role is to ensure not only the adoption of technological solutions, but also their correct implementation, technical monitoring, and systematic recording of their effectiveness.

## *Predictive Sensors and Algorithms*

The use of smart sensors and predictive algorithms represents one of the most significant innovations at the intersection of technology and occupational health. These devices, coupled to machines, clothing, or environments, are capable of collecting real-time data on variables such as temperature, humidity, noise levels, toxic gas concentration, and the worker's heart rate. Schwab (2016, p.125) states that "digital sensors integrated into the internet of things allow continuous surveillance of working conditions, anticipating risks and enabling immediate interventions*. This is a paradigmatic turn, as it shifts the focus of institutional action from a reactive logic - based on punishment after the damage - to a preventive perspective, centered on continuous protection and the anticipation of critical scenarios.

In this sense, the application of predictive algorithms in conjunction with sensors expands the possibilities of managing occupational risks in a strategic and personalized way. The data collected by these devices is processed by artificial intelligence-based systems, capable of identifying patterns and anticipating adverse events, such as thermal collapses, mechanical failures, or prolonged exposure to unhealthy agents. Harari (2018, p.151) points out that "algorithms, when trained with adequate data, can predict not only economic trends, but also critical physiological conditions, intervening before the damage materializes". Such an approach, instead of replacing human supervision, should serve as an ally in immediate decision-making and in the construction of safer, more efficient, and humanized work environments.

The effectiveness of sensors and algorithms in preventing accidents depends, however, on the quality and integrity of the data processed. The massive collection of information must be accompanied by validation, cross-referencing and anonymization mechanisms, in order to avoid interpretative biases that compromise decision-making. Souza (2022, p.91) warns that "predictive intelligence is only useful if it is fed by reliable, calibrated, and ethically collected data; otherwise, it can induce serious errors in the management of occupational health and safety". Thus, information governance becomes a strategic dimension of technological policy in companies, and it is necessary to balance innovation with privacy, efficiency with institutional responsibility. Schwab (2016) corroborates this idea by arguing that algorithmic transparency and ethical oversight are indispensable conditions for social trust in emerging technologies.

By broadening the discussion, it is highlighted that sensors can also act in monitoring the physical exhaustion of the worker, measuring fatigue levels, body temperature and repetitive movements that increase the risk of musculoskeletal injuries. Ferreira (2022, p.80) observes that "the use of fatigue sensors can alert the employer to the need for breaks, redistribution of tasks, or even preventive leave, reducing the incidence of occupational diseases".

These data, when interpreted by algorithms trained on historical databases, provide relevant indicators for preventive health management. Harari

(2018) adds that the ability to interpret biological signals in real time inaugurates a new logic of protection centered on the individual and not only on the environment, which represents an evolution in occupational safety engineering.

Therefore, it is considered that, in the context of the work environment, this predictive capacity not only improves safety, but also serves as an instrument of objective evidence in eventual lawsuits and, in this way, companies that adopt such technologies, when they demonstrate their continuous and effective application, through auditable records and reports, strengthen their position in labor lawsuits. In these situations, judicial experts, when analyzing the data and verifying the effective operation of the sensors, often conclude that there is no unhealthiness.

It is important to emphasize that the mere existence of the equipment is not enough: it is necessary to prove its proper functioning and effective risk mitigation and, therefore, the technology needs to be included in a structured occupational health and safety policy, with documentary and technical support that supports the company's preventive action. From a legal point of view, the admissibility of data obtained through sensors and algorithms will depend on the chain of custody of the information and its technical consistency. When the principles of transparency, traceability, and reliability are respected, these resources can be considered legitimate means of evidence, assisting both in business defense and in judicial decision-making.

## National/International Case Studies and Experiences

The analysis of practical cases and experiences, both national and international, allows us to understand how the application of artificial intelligence (AI) in work environments has been effective in mitigating risks related to unhealthiness. Countries such as Japan and Germany have been standing out in the adoption of automated systems in high-risk sectors, such as mining and the petrochemical industry. Schwab (2016, p.147) reports that: "in Germany, smart factories use sensors and algorithms to automatically adapt production to the detected risk, preserving the physical integrity of workers". This model, based on cyber-physical networks, provides safer work environments, without compromising productivity. In Brazil, although still at an early stage, initiatives in sectors such as agribusiness and the chemical industry are already showing promising advances, especially with the use of drones and ground robots for tasks previously performed by humans in unsanitary conditions.

To broaden this analysis, it is pertinent to look at the experience of South Korea, where the use of AI was incorporated into risk management in hospital and industrial environments. Autonomous robots equipped with thermal and gas sensors are used to inspect hard-to-reach places, preventing direct exposure of workers to pathogens and volatile chemicals. Harari (2018, p.153) observes that the combination of sensors and artificial intelligence enables immediate responses to environmental changes, protecting lives and optimizing production processes*. This experience reinforces the importance of synergy between technological innovation and public policies for occupational safety. In Brazil, initiatives such as those of the Social Service of Industry (SESI) have sought to adapt these practices to the national context, promoting the installation of sensors in manufacturing plants for real-time monitoring of heat, noise and particulate matter.

The consolidation of automated practices in the international logistics sector also illustrates how AI has been employed to minimize ergonomic and biomechanical risks in repetitive and physically demanding tasks. In the case of Amazon, in the United States, robots are used to transport and separate goods in large distribution centers, reducing human effort and exposure to accidents with forklifts and heavy loads. Souza (2022, p.97) points out that "logistics automation not only increases operational efficiency, but also significantly decreases the number of leaves due to musculoskeletal injuries among workers". In Brazil, medium and large companies have been investing in similar technologies, albeit in an incipient way, demonstrating that the practical application of AI in favor of workers' health requires tax incentives, technical training, and an organizational culture focused on prevention.

It is important to note that, in these contexts, the success of business defense is directly related to the company's ability to document and demonstrate the effectiveness of the measures adopted, and it is certain that the absence of reliable records or the inadequate maintenance of systems can compromise the credibility of technical evidence, generating the risk of convictions even in the face of the use of advanced technology.

# THE PROTECTION OF WORKERS' HEALTH IN FLORIDA (USA) AND THE ABSENCE OF THE CONCEPT OF "UNHEALTHINESS" IN THE BRAZILIAN SENSE

## OVERVIEW OF OCCUPATIONAL HEALTH AND SAFETY IN THE UNITED STATES

The North American system of protection of workers' health has as its central milestone the enactment of the Occupational Safety and Health Act of 1970, which broke with the fragmented logic of protection that existed until then and established a national policy aimed at ensuring safe and healthy working conditions through the combination of mandatory standards, inspection, incentive to federative cooperation and promotion of research, education and information in occupational safety and health. He comprehensively structured the duties of employers and the institutional architecture of the public policy for the prevention of occupational accidents and diseases in the United States (United States, 1970).

By summarizing the content of the OSH Act, the institutional synthesis prepared by the federal environmental agency highlights that the law now requires employers to offer an environment free of recognized hazards, such as toxic substances, infectious agents, excessive noise, mechanical hazards, heat stress and other conditions capable of causing death or serious damage, while attributing to the federal government powers to issue technical standards, carry out inspections, impose penalties and support states in the construction of their own safety and health systems, evidencing the North American option for a model centered on risk management and not on the granting of additional remuneration due to exposure to harmful agents, as occurs in the Brazilian model of unhealthiness (United States Environmental Protection Agency, 2025).

Also according to this summary, the OSH Act instituted a set of substantive rights for workers, including the right to a safe workplace, to information about chemical and physical hazards, to receive training in understandable language and form, as well as the right to lodge complaints with the competent authority and to participate in inspections, at the same time, it reinforced the correlated duty of employees to observe applicable safety standards, creating a system in which the responsibility for health protection is shared, but legally anchored in the employer's primary duty to eliminate or control occupational risks (United States Environmental Protection Agency, 2025).

From this legal basis, the brochure "OSHA: All About OSHA" describes the creation and specific role of the Occupational Safety and Health Administration as the agency responsible for the development and enforcement of federal occupational safety and health standards. The material explains that OSHA is organized into national, regional and local offices, with a cadre of inspectors and technical specialists in charge of developing standards, conducting inspections, responding to complaints, promoting education programs and encouraging the adoption of safety management systems, all under the logic that accident prevention is a legal duty and also an element of economic efficiency for companies (Occupational Safety and Health Administration, 2024a).

The same manual emphasizes that OSHA's work combines coercive and cooperative instruments, since, in addition to being able to apply citations and fines in case of non-compliance with the rules, the agency operates voluntary compliance programs, offers educational materials, maintains service lines to clarify doubts and also recognizes companies with exemplary programs. Thus, the North American panorama is characterized by a robust regulatory apparatus aimed at reducing risks at the source and not on the mere financial compensation of workers for exposure to unhealthy environments. This shows a significant conceptual departure from the unhealthy bonus provided for in Brazilian legislation (Occupational Safety and Health Administration, 2024a).

From the perspective of the Department of Labor, the field of safety and health at work is presented as part of a broader agenda for worker protection, in which the application of the OSH Act is articulated with other inspection programs, technical assistance and promotion of good practices, emphasizing that the effective protection of the physical and mental integrity of workers is directly associated with productivity, competitiveness and the reduction of the overall costs of the system, as occupational accidents and diseases generate loss of production, medical expenses, and relevant economic impacts for employers and society (United States Department of Labor, 2024b).

The general panorama described by the Department of Labor itself shows that, more than fifty years after the enactment of the OSH Act, the occupational safety and health policy in the United States remains in constant evolution, with continuous updating of standards, development of sectoral campaigns, centralization of statistical data and dissemination of practical guides for companies of different sizes. The American policy in this area reflects a vision in which risk reduction is treated as a strategic investment and in which regulatory compliance is not limited to avoiding sanctions, but is linked to the construction of more stable, inclusive, and sustainable work environments (United States Department of Labor, 2024b).

In this institutional arrangement, the National Institute for Occupational Safety and Health assumes a complementary role to that of OSHA, since, according to its own institutional presentation, it was created as a research and technical recommendations body, responsible for producing scientific knowledge, developing risk assessment methods, proposing occupational exposure limits and supporting, based on evidence, the elaboration of standards and public policies. It functions as a scientific pillar of a regulatory system that seeks to base its decisions on empirical data on occupational diseases and accidents (National Institute for Occupational Safety and Health, 2024a).

The document "About NIOSH" also clarifies that the institute works through specialized centers, collaborations with universities and partnerships with states and other countries, in addition to developing programs for training professionals and disseminating information, which reinforces the idea that the North American panorama of occupational health goes beyond mere inspection. It incorporates a dimension of applied research and dissemination of knowledge that continuously feeds the updating of prevention practices in the various economic sectors (National Institute for Occupational Safety and Health, 2024a).

Thus, when one observes the OSH Act together, OSHA's normative and supervisory performance, the integrated vision of the Department of Labor, and the scientific support provided by NIOSH, it is clear that the general panorama of occupational health and safety in the United States is structured as a risk management system whose main focus is on eliminating or controlling hazards in the workplace. in order to ensure a "safe and healthy workplace" as a basic right, which makes it clear that the axis of the model is not the attribution of an additional salary for unhealthiness, but the legal obligation to prevent risk, as outlined in the original text of the 1970 law (United States, 1970).

# ENFORCEMENT OF THE OSH ACT AND OSHA STANDARDS IN FLORIDA

The Department of Labor's guide to the Occupational Safety and Health Act and OSHA standards explains that federal law coverage extends to private employers in all states and territories, including Florida, so that in the absence of an approved state plan of their own, Floridian employers remain subject directly to federal OSHA's jurisdiction, and must comply with the safety and health standards applicable to their industries and observe the general duty clause that requires the maintenance of a workplace free from recognized hazards that may cause death or serious physical injury to employees (United

States Department of Labor, 2024a).

This same guide details that, in the Floridian context, the application of the OSH Act implies compliance with a set of rules codified in the Code of Federal Regulations, covering requirements for machine protection, fall prevention, control of chemical agents, order and cleanliness, personal protective equipment, ergonomics and other specific requirements, and that the inspection is conducted by federal inspectors who can initiate an inspection by sectoral programming, by complaints from workers or by the occurrence of serious accidents, and non-compliance results in citations and penalties that can be significant, which directly links the risk management adopted by Florida companies to the federal requirements of OSHA (United States Department of Labor, 2024a).

OSHA's state plan document explains that the OSH Act is designed to encourage states to develop their own occupational safety and health systems, as long as they offer protection "at least as effective" as the federal one, describing that there are currently dozens of approved plans that cover private and public sector workers entirely or focus only on state and local employees. It also clarifies that these plans are jointly funded by fèderal and state resources, and are supervised by OSHA itself to ensure equivalence of protection, which constitutes the benchmark for any Florida initiative to implement its own plan (Occupational Safety and Health Administration, 2024b).

Also according to the text on State Plans, the approval of a state plan requires the presentation of a detailed proposal with an implementation schedule, standards that replicate or exceed federal standards, an inspection structure, an accident registration and reporting system, and stable funding commitments, as well as a transition period in which OSHA continues to act in parallel until the state program demonstrates its ability to ensure adequate protection. This indicates that the political discussion in Florida about assuming its own jurisdiction in matters of occupational safety and health involves not only ideological options, but also the administrative and financial capacity of the state to set up a structure equivalent to the federal one (Occupational Safety and Health Administration, 2024b).

In the context of this discussion, the final analysis of bill HB 5B by the Florida House of Representatives reports that the proposal passed in special session directed that the Executive Office of the Governor prepare a proposal for a state plan for occupational safety and health with the objective of claiming state jurisdiction over occupational safety issues for public and private employees. It also describes the obligation to involve several state agencies in the preparation of the plan and to present, within a defined period, a report to the Legislature containing diagnosis, alternatives, and recommendations, which made explicit the political interest in reassessing the exclusive dependence on federal OSHA (Florida House of Representatives, 2021).

The same HB 5B analysis highlights that the project provided specific resources for the development of the plan, indicated that the proposal should detail the form of financing the program, the inspection structure, the initial priorities for action and the relationship with federal standards, in addition to mentioning that the creation of a state plan approved by OSHA would put Florida in a position similar to that of other states that already exercise their own authority over Occupational safety.

It was implied that this movement could be used politically to reinforce state autonomy, although the requirement of equivalence of protection limits any attempts to make standards more flexible in relation to the federal level (Florida House of Representatives, 2021).

Parallel to the discussion on a state plan, Chapter 442 of the Florida Statutes establishes the state's own legal framework for occupational safety and health, indicating the legislative intention to promote the prevention of work-related accidents and diseases. In addition, it defines competencies for inspections, consultations and studies on occupational risks and provides for the possibility of adopting rules and mechanisms for cooperation with insurers and self-insured persons, so that, still under the aegis of the federal OSHA, the state has its own legal instruments to promote safety programs and to study health problems for workers in its territory (Florida, 2000).

The same chapter 442 also regulates the formation of safety committees, the role of the competent division in carrying out investigations into occupational accidents and diseases, the responsibility of employers to adopt protective measures and the possibility of establishing rules on inspections and consultations. This demonstrates that Florida has built a normative framework that, although it does not replace OSHA's jurisdiction over the private sector, works as a complement aimed mainly at the organization of prevention at the state level, with special emphasis on public work environments and on the coordination of inspection and education efforts (Florida, 2000).

The practical application of this arrangement in Florida is also materialized through the physical presence of OSHA in the state, as the list of Florida OSHA Area Offices indicates the existence of regional offices that serve employers and workers in strategic cities, responsible for conducting inspections, responding to complaints, offering lectures and acting as points of contact for the clarification of regulatory doubts, which brings the federal structure closer to the daily life of Floridian companies. In addition, it contributes to the implementation of federal standards being sensitive to the sectoral and geographic particularities of the state (Occupational Safety and Health Administration, 2024c).

In this context, the very description of OSHA's area offices in Florida reinforces that these agencies function as a gateway both for inspection and for the provision of educational resources and cooperation programs, indicating contact numbers, addresses and channels for scheduling actions, so that the application of the OSH Act and OSHA standards in the state is achieved by the combination of a federal legal apparatus, complementary state legislation and local administrative structures. These connect the regulatory authority to the reality of Floridian workplaces in a model in which protection is not expressed by additional remuneration, but by the requirement of technical compliance with detailed safety and health standards (Occupational

Safety and Health Administration, 2024c).

Finally, the picture described by OSHA on state plans shows that, as long as there is no approval of its own plan that meets the criterion of equivalent effectiveness, Florida remains a state under full federal jurisdiction, although with its own statutes that deal with safety at work and legislative initiatives such as HB 5B seeking to redesign this relationship. Thus, the protection of workers' health in the state results from the interaction between mandatory federal standards, OSHA inspection structures installed in Floridian territory and complementary state rules, without instituting an additional unhealthy work allowance in the mold of Brazilian law as a central protection mechanism (Occupational Safety and Health Administration, 2024b).

# FLORIDA'S OWN LAWS AND POLICIES RELATED TO OCCUPATIONAL HEALTH

In the field of compensation for damages arising from accidents and occupational diseases, Chapter 440 of the Florida Statutes constitutes the main normative basis. It regulates the workers' compensation system and establishes that covered employers must ensure benefits to employees who suffer work-related injuries or illnesses. This reveals that state legal protection is organized based on a mandatory insurance regime, aimed at guaranteeing medical care and income replacement, instead of structuring a general unhealthy surcharge linked to mere exposure to harmful agents, as occurs in the Brazilian model (Florida, 2024).

This chapter details, among other things, the requirements for coverage, the obligations to take out insurance or to maintain self-insurance programs, the definitions of accident and occupational disease, as well as the rules on reporting events, deadlines, and procedures for claiming benefits, so that the Floridian compensation system focuses on repairing and managing the costs of work-related injuries. integrating occupational health policy through economic incentives for prevention, to the extent that accidents and injuries directly impact the cost of insurance and the employer's financial responsibility (Florida, 2024).

The "Workers' Compensation Laws and Rules" compendium, prepared by the Workers' Compensation Division of the Department of Financial Services, organizes and updates the laws and regulations related to workers' compensation. It also provides a systematized view of Chapter 440 provisions, supplemental administrative rules, and practical guidance for employers, insurers, and legal professionals, which facilitates understanding of legal obligations and reinforces the system's role as a central instrument for managing economic risks associated with occupational health in Florida (Florida Department of Financial Services, 2024).

This material highlights that the workers' compensation system establishes medical, rehabilitation, and income replacement benefits, as well as mechanisms for resolving conflicts and penalties for non-compliance with coverage obligations. In addition, it provides for programs that can reduce premiums for employers who adopt effective prevention practices, which highlights the logic that more robust safety policies have a direct impact on the reduction of insurance costs, reinforcing a model in which prevention is related to economic incentives and in which the health hazard bonus is not used as the main instrument of protection (Florida Department of Financial Services, 2024).

In the field of health surveillance, the Occupational Health Surveillance section of the Occupational Health and Safety Program, coordinated by the Florida Department of Health, describes that the program is responsible for monitoring work-related health conditions, identifying trends in occupational diseases and injuries, and producing information capable of guiding public policies, with the objective of reducing the incidence of work-related injuries through evidence-based actions and targeting higher-risk sectors and groups (Florida Department of Health, 2023).

According to this presentation, occupational health surveillance uses a variety of data sources, such as records of hospital admissions, notifications of occupational diseases, information from the workers' compensation system, and mortality reports, integrating these databases to identify risk patterns, map the most affected economic sectors, and support prevention programs. This demonstrates that Florida uses epidemiological surveillance as a structuring component of its occupational health policy (Florida Department of Health, 2023).

The Florida Occupational Health and Safety Program's fact sheet brochure highlights that the program is funded in part by federal funds and is part of a broader network of occupational health programs supported by NIOSH, outlining goals such as reducing occupational deaths and injuries, preventing exposure-related illnesses, and strengthening partnerships with regulatory agencies. employers and workers. In this way, the state seeks to transform surveillance data into concrete actions for prevention, education, and change of practices in work environments (Florida Department of Health, 2020).

This material also summarizes strategic priorities such as the monitoring of high-risk sectors, the investigation of outbreaks or sentinel events, the development of educational materials and technical guidance for the adoption of preventive measures, which reinforces that, from the point of view of public health, the state occupational health policy is oriented to the early identification of problems and intervention on their causes. in addition to the legal compensation system provided for in Chapter 440 (Florida Department of Health, 2020).

The program's communiqués that release reports on work-related deaths and the economic costs of these occurrences show that Florida tracks occupational mortality indicators and estimates the financial impact of accidents and illnesses, highlighting that fatal work events represent not only human tragedies, but also significant economic losses for families, employers, and the state itself, which reinforces the need for robust preventive policies and strategies focused on the sectors at greatest risk (Florida Department of Health, 2022).

In releasing these reports, the occupational health program also draws attention to the concentration of certain types of events in sectors such as construction, transportation, and agriculture. It also draws attention to the importance of considering demographic and social factors in understanding occupational health inequalities, in order to guide targeted interventions, which demonstrates an evidence-based public policy approach aimed at reducing risks in Floridian work environments (Florida Department of Health, 2022).

Taken together, the compensation regime provided for in Chapter 440 and the surveillance and intervention strategies of the occupational health program make up a framework in which Florida protects the health of workers based on insurance redress and epidemiological monitoring mechanisms, articulated with technical safety standards, without resorting to an additional general remuneration for unhealthiness, privileging risk management, economic accountability for damages, and the use of data to guide prevention and inspection policies (Florida, 2024).

## GUIDELINES AND PROGRAMS FOR BUSINESSES IN FLORIDA

OSHA's brochure on the On-Site Consultation Program explains that this program provides free and confidential occupational safety and health consulting services to small and medium-sized businesses, with priority given to those operating in higher-risk sectors, noting that the initiative is funded by federal resources in cooperation with states and aims to help employers identify hazards. improve their prevention programs and achieve compliance with applicable regulations, without being directly linked to the application of fines or citations (Occupational Safety and Health Administration, 2024d).

The same document clarifies that, by requesting the consultancy, the employer is committed to correcting the serious risks identified within agreed deadlines, but benefits from a collaborative approach in which experts visit the workplace, analyze processes, review written programs and offer practical recommendations for improvements, which contributes to smaller Floridian companies being able to implement higher safety and health standards even without having them of large internal risk management structure (Occupational Safety and Health Administration, 2024d).

Other OSHA material, presented under the motto "Safety and Health Advice You Can Trust for Your Small Business," emphasizes that small businesses often face specific barriers in implementing safety programs, such as limitations on financial and technical resources, and that the consulting program provides reliable guidance on identifying hazards, selecting control measures, and complying with regulatory requirements. reinforcing that the prevention of accidents and illnesses is not only a legal obligation, but also a strategy for reducing costs, protecting the workforce, and strengthening business reputation (Occupational Safety and Health Administration, 2024e).

This material also highlights that the consultancy can assist in the preparation or review of written programs required by OSHA standards, in carrying out environmental measurements, in evaluating the use of personal protective equipment and in building a culture of participatory safety, stimulating the formation of internal committees, communication about risks and the integration of safety into daily management processes, which reveals that the North American policy combines the imposition of mandatory minimum standards with technical support mechanisms that seek to raise the average level of protection in companies, including those based in Florida (Occupational Safety and Health Administration, 2024e).

At the state level, the SafetyFlorida overview presents the program as the occupational safety and health consulting arm administered by the University of South Florida through a cooperative agreement with OSHA, explaining that the initiative offers risk assessment services, helps in the implementation of prevention programs, and supports compliance with federal standards, with a special focus on small and medium-sized businesses that want to improve their safety performance without waiting for an inspection to arrive (University of South Florida, 2023a).

According to the description of the SafetyFlorida Consultation Program, the program's teams conduct on-site visits to companies throughout the state, identify hazards in machinery, electrical installations, confined spaces, ergonomics and exposure to chemical agents, discuss source control, administrative and personal protection solutions, and prepare reports with recommendations and implementation deadlines, maintaining the confidentiality of the information and only reporting to OSHA situations in which the employer does not comply with the commitments made, which reinforces the cooperative and educational nature of the initiative (University of South Florida, 2023b).

The "About Us" section of SafetyFlorida informs that the program has been operating for decades in Florida and that its consultants have training in several technical areas, such as occupational hygiene, construction safety, ergonomics and electrical safety, emphasizing that the institutional mission is to reduce injuries, illnesses and fatalities at work through partnerships with employers, unions, industry associations and educational entities, in order to disseminate a culture of prevention that goes beyond mere formal compliance with OSHA standards (University of South Florida, 2023c).

One of the case studies presented by the program reports the experience of the company Portside Maintenance and Repair, showing that, with the support of SafetyFlorida consultants, the organization identified significant risks in port maintenance operations, related to falls, cargo handling, noise exposure and improper use of protective equipment. It has also implemented improvements such as the installation of physical barriers, review of work procedures, intensification of training, and adoption of engineering controls, resulting in a reduction in incidents and strengthening of the safety culture (University of South Florida, 2021).

The report highlights that, in addition to the technical changes, the company started to document its safety actions more systematically, establish performance indicators and involve workers in identifying hazards and proposing solutions. This demonstrates how consulting programs can transform the way risk management is perceived internally, from being a mere external requirement to being a constituent element of business management, aligned with federal and state regulatory expectations in Florida (University of South Florida, 2021).

In this way, the combination of OSHA's On-Site Consultation Program and the local performance of SafetyFlorida creates an environment in which Floridian companies have consistent technical support to implement occupational safety and health standards, reinforcing the understanding that worker health protection is achieved by anticipating and controlling risks, by building management programs and continuously improving safety performance, and not simply granting an unhealthy allowance as financial compensation for hazardous environments (University of South Florida, 2023a).

# ARTIFICIAL INTELLIGENCE, RISK MONITORING, AND REGULATORY COMPLIANCE IN FLORIDA

John Howard's article on the implications of artificial intelligence for the future of work presents AI as a general-purpose technology that, like the steam engine or electricity in other historical periods, has the potential to profoundly transform the organization of production, work tasks, and risk patterns. The article also highlights that applications based on machine learning, smart sensors, robotics, and decision support systems already permeate numerous work environments and that these changes can both reduce certain hazards and create new types of risks. This requires the occupational safety and health area to develop capacities to anticipate scenarios, rather than just react to consummated accidents (Howard, 2019).

In the same text, Howard argues that the diffusion of AI in workplaces can impact mental workload, worker autonomy, digital surveillance, and the distribution of tasks between humans and machines, raising questions about job displacement, intensification of the pace of work, and possible failures of automated systems, and maintains that a responsible approach to safety and health should incorporate prospective analyses on these impacts, so that employers and regulators can shape the adoption of smart technologies in ways that maximize benefits and minimize harm to workers' physical and mental health, including in states like Florida where compliance with OSHA standards remains the lynchpin of protection (Howard, 2019).

Shah's review on artificial intelligence in occupational safety and health highlights that AI-based technologies are revolutionizing the way organizations approach prevention by enabling real-time monitoring, early identification of risk patterns, and the development of predictive models capable of anticipating accident and disease events. showing that algorithms applied to large volumes of data from environmental sensors, wearable devices, and administrative records can assist in prioritizing interventions and allocating prevention resources more efficiently (Shah, 2024).

This study emphasizes that the L can be used to analyze historical series of occurrences, identify combinations of risk factors frequently present before serious accidents, and suggest modifications in work processes or equipment design. In addition, it can support the early diagnosis of occupational diseases through the analysis of imaging tests and other clinical data, which opens the door for companies subject to Florida legislation to incorporate intelligent monitoring tools as part of their OSHA compliance programs and to reduce costs associated with accidents and illnesses (Shah, 2024).

The proposal for the REDECA framework, presented by Pishgar et al., offers a specific conceptual framework to relate artificial intelligence and occupational health and safety, by organizing the risk management cycle into stages of evolution, detection, evaluation, and control of accidents, and showing how different AI techniques can support each of these phases. from identifying changes in operating patterns that indicate increased risk to selecting the most appropriate control strategies to eliminate hazards or reduce exposures to acceptable levels (Pishgar, 2021). In the study in which REDECA is presented, the authors analyze hundreds of applications of IA in sectors such as oil and gas, mining, transportation, construction, and agriculture, showing that most experiments focus on the use of sensors to detect dangerous situations, the monitoring of behaviors, and the automation of tasks in hostile environments. The authors argue that this type of structured approach helps identify research gaps and opportunities for developing more comprehensive solutions, which is relevant for states such as Florida, which have a strong presence of high-risk sectors and can benefit from the orderly incorporation of L.A. technologies into prevention programs (Pishgar, 2021).

The study by Kulinan and co-authors on workforce safety monitoring on construction sites through the integration between BIM and computer vision describes the development of a system that combines closed-circuit camera images with building information models, using object detection algorithms to identify workers, classify the use of personal protective equipment and project the position of workers in the BIM model, so as to allow near-real-time visualization of unsafe situations and subsequent analysis of historical data to improve safety planning on construction sites (Kulinan, 2024). According to this work, the application of computer vision and BIM allowed the creation of a "safety twin" of the site, in which managers can observe the movement of workers, verify that helmets and vests are being used and identify areas with a higher concentration of risk behaviors, paving the way for companies in the construction industry, including in Florida, to employ similar tools to document compliance with regulatory requirements, justify safety-oriented design decisions, and support due diligence demonstrations in inspection or workers' compensation processes (Kulinan, 2024).

The Center for Occupational Robotics Research website, maintained by NIOSH, presents a research agenda specifically focused on the safety of workers who use, wear, or work near robots, indicating that the center monitors injury trends associated with robotic technologies, evaluates robots as potential sources of risk, and also as possible interventions to reduce human exposures. defines risk profiles of robotic environments and participates in the development of safety standards for different types of robotics, including collaborative robots, autonomous vehicles, and exoskeletons, many of them integrating advanced artificial intelligence components (National Institute for Occupational Safety and Health, 2024b).

This document emphasizes that the center works in partnership with other agencies and OSHA itself to develop guidelines, identify research needs, and disseminate good practices for safe human-robot interaction, recognizing that the introduction of robotic and AI technologies in workplaces must be accompanied by systematic risk assessments, updates to technical standards and specific training programs, which is particularly relevant for states such as Florida, which have intensive sectors in logistics, ports, mechanized agriculture, and construction, all of which are susceptible to rapid automation (National Institute for Occupational Safety and Health, 2024b).

By articulating Howard's reflections on the future of work with empirical evidence on applications of AI in occupational health and institutional initiatives aimed at safety in robotic environments, it becomes possible to envision a scenario in which Floridian employers, subject to the requirements of the OSH Act and OSHA standards, start to use intelligent systems to monitor exposures, detect risk behaviors, document regulatory compliance, and support engineering and work organization decisions, provided that these technologies are implemented with attention to ethical, privacy, and worker participation issues, otherwise they will become new sources of illness and conflict rather than instruments for promoting safer work environments (Howard, 2019).

# CONCLUSION

This work, under a descriptive-argumentative approach, analyzed the impact of Artificial Intelligence (AI) in mitigating unhealthy conditions in work environments, especially in sectors historically marked by exposure to harmful agents, such as mining, civil construction, heavy industry and urban cleaning services. Throughout the analysis, it was possible to verify that AI, when implemented in an ethical, regulated, and technically oriented way, represents a transformative vector for the restructuring of the world of work with a focus on health, safety, and human dignity.

Intelligent automation, combined with monitoring sensors, predictive algorithms and risk management platforms, allows a redesign of work functions. Thus, it distances human beings from the most dangerous, repetitive and degrading tasks. This leave not only preserves the physical integrity of workers, but also contributes to the appreciation of work and to the reduction of judicialization resulting from exposure to unhealthy environments.

It was possible to conclude that the use of AI-based technologies does not fully replace the workforce, but reconfigures it, repositioning the worker as an agent of control, supervision and qualification. This functional displacement requires policies of continuous training and requalification, in order to prevent the technological transition from expanding social inequalities that already exist in the Brazilian labor market.

Likewise, it is verified that the IA has a relevant role in the sphere of the Labor Courts, especially by allowing greater procedural speed, precision in the production of expert evidence and effectiveness in the remote inspection of working conditions. The experience of the Victor system, implemented in the Federal Supreme Court, offers replicability parameters for labor courts by demonstrating that the use of algorithms can contribute to a more resolutive and preventive judicial action.

In addition, AI has enormous potential to subsidize public policies aimed at occupational health. The continuous collection of environmental data and the real-time analysis of variables such as temperature, noise and the presence of toxic agents offer inspection agencies strategic information for immediate action, overcoming the historical structural limitations of labor inspection in Brazil.

However, the study recognizes that the incorporation of the law in the workplace and in the Labor Courts is not without risks and, therefore, issues such as data protection, algorithmic transparency, discriminatory biases and the absence of specific regulation were identified as ethical and legal obstacles that need to be urgently addressed by the responsible institutions. The absence of a robust legal framework that disciplines the use of LA in work contexts compromises legal certainty and can open the door to the abusive use of these technologies to the detriment of the fundamental rights of workers. Thus, it is essential that Labor Law keeps up with the pace of technological innovation without renouncing its founding principles.

In this work, the formulation of a hybrid regulation capable of guaranteeing security, innovation and social justice is proposed. This regulation must be built in dialogue with workers, employers, unions, technology specialists and public institutions, in order to contemplate the specificities of each productive sector and ensure the full protection of workers' health.

It was also evidenced that AI can be an ally in the implementation of the Sustainable Development Goals of the UN 2030 Agenda, especially goals 8 and 9, which deal with decent work and innovation. Technology, if used responsibly, can contribute to reducing social inequality and promoting safer and more inclusive work environments.

Undoubtedly, AI has the potential to transform the organizational culture of companies. The adoption of smart technologies, when guided by ethical guidelines and accompanied by adequate technical training, can induce structural changes in the way organizations manage health and safety, migrating from reactive models to preventive and sustainable strategies. In this process, the Labor Courts assume a strategic role as an agent of mediation between innovation and social rights, whose performance can boost a culture of preventive protection by encouraging the adoption of good technological practices and holding employers accountable for neglecting safety standards in unhealthy environments.

It is essential to highlight that the technology is not neutral and its impact will depend on the context in which it is implemented. As argued by Schwab (2016) and Harari (2018), the way societies regulate and integrate technological innovations will determine whether they will be tools of liberation or oppression. This ethical dilemma permeated the entire analysis carried out here. In this sense, the need for continuous training of legal operators, safety engineers, public managers and technology professionals becomes evident, so that they understand the risks, limitations and potentialities of AI.

The analysis reinforces that the confrontation of unhealthiness can no longer dispense with the strategic use of intelligent technologies, and it is certain that traditional solutions are insufficient in the face of contemporary challenges, and innovation, as long as it is guided by ethical and constitutional principles, is a necessary way to ensure health, justice and dignity at work. On the practical level, the analysis contained in this work can serve as a subsidy for the elaboration of public policies aimed at the protection of workers' health, for the modernization of the normative apparatus on unhealthiness, as well as to assist companies in structuring safe, efficient and healthy work environments. The improvement of the mechanisms of inspection and judicial action should also be considered.

Finally, it is reaffirmed that Artificial Intelligence should not be understood as a substitute for human beings, but as an ally in the process of humanizing work, whose responsible use can reduce risks, expand protections and strengthen social rights, as long as it is conducted under the primacy of justice and equity.

It is observed that AI represents a concrete opportunity to transform the work environment into a safer, more dignified and efficient space, but, above all, for this transformation to be fully carried out, a collective commitment to democratic regulation, transparency and respect for the centrality of the human being in the construction of a fairer work future is necessary.

In addition, it is essential to recognize that the judgment of labor lawsuits involving unhealthiness cannot be guided by generic presumptions or interpretative automatisms. The existence of environments with potential biological risk, such as collective bathrooms, for example, requires concrete analysis based on expert evidence duly carried out by a qualified professional. Despite the prevailing jurisprudence, especially after the issuance of Precedent 448 of the TST, it guides the performance of judges, but does not suppress the need for technical and individualized evaluation in each case.

The performance of judicial expertise presents itself as a decisive tool for the outcome of the demands. Effective measures by employers, such as automated toilets, hygiene protocols, and the use of predictive technologies, can rule out the characterization of unhealthiness. It is at this point that Labor Law, combined with technology, finds a fertile field of rationalization and balance between worker protection and legal certainty for the employer.

Thus, it is concluded that the advancement of artificial intelligence in the workplace, combined with the production of qualified technical evidence, not only contributes to the construction of safer and more modern environments, but also strengthens corporate defense mechanisms, when used with responsibility, transparency and commitment to workers' health.

It should not be forgotten, moreover, that the analysis compared with the United States, based on the Florida perspective, shows that the protection of workers' health can follow different normative and institutional paths, without losing sight of the common objective of protecting human dignity at work. While the Brazilian model historically associates unhealthiness with technical-legal characterization and compensation (as well as with the intense litigiousness and centrality of expert evidence), the North American context tends to emphasize safety standards, employer preventive duties, inspection, and regulatory compliance, which shifts the debate to continuous prevention strategies.

Artificial Intelligence can reduce or eliminate unhealthiness, reduce business costs with the payment of additional remuneration provided for in Brazilian legislation, anticipate risks, and contribute to faster judicial decisions. At this point, Artificial Intelligence emerges as a possible bridge between models: it can qualify risk management, strengthen preventive actions, and produce more consistent technical evidence, reducing exposure to harmful agents before the damage consolidates. Thus, the Florida perspective not only complements the study, but reinforces the need to rethink, in a critical and responsible way, how technology, regulation, and public policies can converge to safer work environments, with greater protective effectiveness and less dependence on merely reparatory responses.

# REFERENCES

Alcantara, Igor. (2023). The Ethics of Artificial Intelligence in the Workplace. Linkedin. Publicação em Rede Social.

Amorin, Ricardo. (2025). Banheiro público em Paris automatizado. Threads, 2025. Publicação em Rede Social Vídeo. Acesso em 17 de julho de 2025, https://www.threads.com/@ricamorim/post/DL5lMK0h65C/video-em-paris-banheiros-p%C3%BAblicos-totalmente-automatizados-realizam-higieniza%C3%A7%C3%A3o-compl

Antunes, Ricardo. (2018). Adeus ao trabalho? Ensaio sobre as metamorfoses e a centralidade do mundo do trabalho. 16. ed. São Paulo: Cortez.

Antunes, Ricardo. (2020). O privilégio da servidão: o novo proletariado de serviços na era digital. 2. ed. São Paulo: Boitempo.

Barros, Alice Monteiro de. (2017). Curso de Direito do Trabalho. 11. ed. São Paulo: Imprenta.

Brasil. Decreto-Lei nº 5.452, de 1º de maio de 1943. Aprova a Consolidação das Leis do Trabalho (CLT). Acesso em 01 de junho de 2025, https://www.planalto.gov.br/ccivil_03/decreto-lei/del5452.htm

Brasil. Decreto-Lei nº 5.452, de 1º de maio de 1943. Aprova a Consolidação das Leis do Trabalho (CLT). Acesso em 01 de junho de 2025, https://www.gov.br/trabalho-e-emprego/pt-br/assuntos/seguranca-e-saude-no-trabalho.

Brasil. Constituição (1988). Constituição da República Federativa do Brasil. Brasília, DF: Presidência da República. Acesso em 01 de junho de 2025, https://www.planalto.gov.br/ccivil_03/constituicao/constituicao.htm

Brasil. Lei nº 8.213, de 24 de julho de 1991. Dispõe sobre os Planos de Benefícios da Previdência Social.

Brasil. Código Civil. Lei nº 10.406, de 10 de janeiro de 2002.

Brasil. Código de Processo Civil. Lei nº 13.105, de 16 de março de 2015.

Brasil. Lei nº 13.467, de 13 de julho de 2017. Reforma Trabalhista.

Brasil. Lei nº 13.709, de 14 de agosto de 2018. Lei Geral de Proteção de Dados (LGPD).

Brasil. Portaria nº 6.730, de 9 de março de 2020. Aprova a nova redação da NR-1.

Brasil. Ministério do Trabalho e Emprego. Nova NR-1: Disposições Gerais. 2020.

Brasil. Senado Federal. Projeto de Lei nº 2.338/2023. Estabelece fundamentos, princípios e diretrizes para o desenvolvimento e a aplicação da inteligência artificial no Brasil.

Brasil. Tribunal Superior do Trabalho. Súmulas. Brasília, DF: Tribunal Superior do Trabalho, s.d. Base de dados jurídica. Acesso em 17 de julho de 2025, https://jurisprudencia.tst.jus.br/?tipoJuris=SUM&orgao=TST&pesquisar=1

Brynjolfsson, Erik; Mcafee, Andrew. (2014). A segunda era das máquinas. Rio de Janeiro: Alta Books.

Cabral, João Pedro Gomes; Rocha, Hudson Ferreira; Souza, Ana Paula Jesus; Oliveira, Danilo da Silva; Lima, Juliano Freire (2024). Direito e tecnologia: o uso da inteligência artificial na Justiça do Trabalho. Revista Foco, 17(12).

Catalini, Christian; Gans, Joshua S. (2020). Some Simple Economics of the Blockchain. MIT Sloan Research Paper.

Dejours, Christophe. (2011). A banalização da injustiça social. 7. ed. Rio de Janeiro: Fundação Getúlio Vargas.

Delgado, Maurício Godinho. (2020). Curso de Direito do Trabalho. 19. ed. São Paulo: LTr.

Domingos, Pedro. (2017). O algoritmo mestre: como a busca por um algoritmo pode mudar o mundo. São Paulo: Novatec.

Doneda, Danilo. (2019). Da privacidade à proteção de dados pessoais: elementos da formação da Lei Geral de Proteção de Dados. Rio de Janeiro: Revista dos Tribunais.

Eubanks, Virginia. (2018). Automating Inequality: How High-Tech Tools Profile, Police, and Punish the Poor. New York: St. Martin's Press.

European Commission. (2021). Proposal for a Regulation laying down harmonised rules on Artificial Intelligence (Artificial Intelligence Act). Brussels.

EU-OSHA - European Agency for Safety and Health at Work. (2021). The impact of artificial intelligence on occupational safety and health. Luxembourg: Publications Office of the European Union.

Ferreira, Geovana Magalhães. (2022). Inteligência artificial como auxiliar do poder judiciário: a experiência do sistema Victor no âmbito do STF [Trabalho de Conclusão de Curso de Graduação, Universidade Federal do Ceará].

Florida. (2000). The 2000 Florida Statutes: Chapter 442 Occupational Safety and Health. Tallahassee.

Florida. (2024). The 2024 Florida Statutes: Chapter 440 Workers' Compensation. Tallahassee.

Florida Department of Financial Services. (2024). Workers' Compensation Laws and Rules. Tallahassee.

Florida Department of Health. (2020). Florida Occupational Health and Safety Program: Fact Sheet. Tallahassee.

Florida Department of Health. (2022). Florida Occupational Health and Safety Program releases reports on work-related fatalities and costs. Tallahassee.

Florida Department of Health. (2023). Occupational Health Surveillance. Tallahassee.

Florida House of Representatives. (2021). HB 5B Florida Occupational Safety and Health State Plan Staff Final Bill Analysis. Tallahassee.

Garcia, Gustavo Filipe Barbosa. (2021). Direito Processual do Trabalho. 16. ed. São Paulo: Método.

Gusmão, Bráulio Gabriel. (2022, jan./jun.) Evolução tecnológica e inteligência artificial na Justiça do Trabalho. Revista do Tribunal Regional do Trabalho da 2ª Região, São Paulo, 14(27), pp. 111-121.

Haenlein, Michael; Kaplan, Andreas. (2019) A brief history of artificial intelligence: On the past, present, and future of artificial intelligence. California Management Review, 61(4).

Harari, Yuval Noah. (2018). 21 lições para o século 21. São Paulo: Companhia das Letras.

Howard, John. (2019). Artificial intelligence: implications for the future of work. American Journal of Industrial Medicine, 62(11), pp. 917-926.

ITATIAIA. (2024). BH terá banheiros públicos ao estilo de Paris; saiba onde serão instalados. Acesso em 17 de julho de 2025, https://www.itatiaia.com.br/cidade-conecta/2024/10/21/bh-tera-banheiros-publicos-ao-estilo-de-paris-saiba-onde-serao-instalados

Jurafsky, Daniel; Martin, James H. (2008). Speech and Language Processing. 3rd ed. Pearson.

Kulinan, Almo Senja; Park, Minsoo; Aung, Pa Pa Win; Cha, Gichun; Park, Seunghee. (2024). Advancing construction site workforce safety monitoring through BIM and computer vision integration. Automation in Construction, 158.

Lee, H.; Yoon, C. (2021). Application of Artificial Intelligence-Based Technologies in the Healthcare Industry: Opportunities and Challenges. National Library os Medicine,18(1).

Leite, Carlos Henrique Bezerra. (2023). Curso de Direito do Trabalho. 15. ed. São Paulo: Saraiva.

Lopes, Eduardo Alcântara; Pivatto, Caio. (2023). Tecnologia na Justiça do Trabalho: o uso das provas digitais. Acesso em 09 de julho de 2025, https://

analise.com/opiniao/tecnologia-na-justica-do-trabalho-o-uso-das-provas-digitais

Machado, Fernanda de Vargas; Colombo, Cristiano. Inteligência artificial aplicada à atividade jurisdicional. (2021). Revista da Escola Judicial do TRT4, [S. l.], 3(5), pp. 117–141.

Ministério do Trabalho e Emprego. Norma Regulamentadora nº. 15 (NR-15). Acesso em 14 de julho de 2025, https://www.gov.br/trabalho-e-emprego/pt-br/acesso-a-informacao/participacao-social/conselhos-e-orgaos-colegiados/comissao-tripartite-partitaria-permanente/normas-regulamentadora/normas-regulamentadoras-vigentes/norma-regulamentadora-no-15-nr-15

Moreira, Samantha Caroline Ferreira; Fernandes, Ricardo Augusto. (2020, out./dez.). A aplicabilidade da inteligência artificial ao processo do trabalho e a segurança jurídica. Revista do Tribunal Superior do Trabalho, 86(4).

MPT – Ministério Público do Trabalho. (2022). Observatório de Segurança e Saúde no Trabalho. Acesso em 01 de junho de 2025, https://smartlabbr.org/sst

National Institute for Occupational Safety and Health. (2024a). About NIOSH. Atlanta.

National Institute for Occupational Safety and Health. (2024b). Center for Occupational Robotics Research. Atlanta.

Occupational Safety and Health Administration. (2024a). OSHA: All About OSHA. Washington, DC.

Occupational Safety and Health Administration. (2024b). State Plans. Washington, DC.

Occupational Safety and Health Administration. (2024c). Florida OSHA Area Offices. Washington, DC.

Occupational Safety and Health Administration. (2024d). On-Site Consultation Program. Washington, DC.

Occupational Safety and Health Administration. (2024e). Safety and Health Advice You Can Trust for Your Small Business. Washington, DC.

OIT – Organização Internacional do Trabalho. (2019). Normas internacionais do trabalho. Genebra: OIT.

OIT – Organização Internacional do Trabalho. (2021). Digital labour platforms and the future of work. Genebra: OIT.

OIT – Organização Internacional do Trabalho. (2025). IA e digitalização estão transformando a segurança e a saúde no trabalho. Acesso em 12 de junho de 2025, https://www.ilo.org/pt-pt/resource/news/ia-e-digitalizacao-estao-transformando-seguranca-e-saude-no-trabalho

Oliveira, Maria Aparecida Rodrigues Oliveira et al. (2023). O impacto da inteligência artificial no mundo do trabalho. Revista Multidisciplinar do Nordeste Mineiro, 12(1).

OMS – Organização Mundial da Saúde. (2022). Mental health at work: policy brief. Genebra: WHO.

Peck, Patrícia. (2021). Direito Digital: O impacto da tecnologia na sociedade e no mundo jurídico. 7. ed. São Paulo: Saraiva.

Pishgar, Maryam; Issa, Salah F.; Sietsema, Margaret; Pratap, Preethi; Darabi, Houshang. REDECA: a novel framework to review artificial intelligence and its applications in occupational safety and health. International Journal of Environmental Research and Public Health, 18(13), pp. 6705, 2021.

Prefeitura de Belo Horizonte. (2025). Prefeitura inaugura primeiro banheiro autolimpante de Belo Horizonte. Acesso em 17 de julho de 2025, https://prefeitura.pbh.gov.br/noticias/prefeitura-inaugura-primeiro-banheiro-autolimpante-de-belo-horizonte

Ramos, Janine Vilas Boas Gonçalves. (2022). Inteligência artificial no Poder Judiciário Brasileiro: projetos de IA nos tribunais e o sistema de apoio ao processo decisório judicial. São Paulo: Dialética.

Russell, Stuart; Norvig, Peter. (2020). Artificial Intelligence: A Modern Approach. 4th ed. New Jersey: Pearson.

SafetyFlorida. (2023). SafetyFlorida: Overview. Tampa.

Santos, Karoline Barbosa. (2025). Da eficiência à ética: o uso de inteligência artificial no Judiciário brasileiro. Acesso em 01 de julho de 2025, https://www.migalhas.com.br/depeso/433321/eficiencia-e-etica-no-uso-da-inteligencia-artificial-no-judiciario. Acesso em: 01 jul. 2025.

Shah, Immad A. (2024). Artificial intelligence in advancing occupational health and safety: an encapsulation of developments. Journal of Occupational Health, 66(1).

SchiavI, Mauro. (2022). Curso de Direito do Trabalho. 18. ed. São Paulo: LTr.

Schwab, Klaus. (2016). A quarta revolução industrial. São Paulo: Edipro.

Secrets os Paris. (n.d.). Banheiros públicos. Acesso em 17 de julho de 2025, https://secretsofparis-com.translate.goog/practical/restrooms/?_x_tr_sl=en&_x_tr_tl=pt&_x_tr_hl=pt&_x_tr_pto=tc

Souza, Adriana Lúcia Muniz de. (2021). A aplicação da inteligência artificial no Poder Judiciário e a eficiência. ENAJUS.

Souza, Rodrigo Lemos de. (2022). Inteligência artificial, trabalho e direitos fundamentais. Belo Horizonte: Fórum.

Souza, Keli Alves de. (2024, abr.). Provas digitais no processo do trabalho: obtenção e utilização pelo magistrado. Revista Eletrônica do TRT-PR. Curitiba: TRT-9ª Região, 13(130).

Susskind, Daniel. (2020). A World Without Work: Technology, Automation, and How We Should Respond. New York: Metropolitan Books.

Toledo, Cláudia; Pessoa, Daniel. (2023). O uso da inteligência artificial na tomada de decisão judicial. Rev. Investig. Const., 10(1).

Topol, Eric. (2019). Deep Medicine: How Artificial Intelligence Can Make Healthcare Human Again. New York: Basic Books.

United States. (1970). Occupational Safety and Health Act of 1970. Washington, DC.

United States Department of Labor. (2024a). Employment Law Guide: Occupational Safety and Health. Washington, DC.

United States Department of Labor. (2024b). Workplace Safety and Health. Washington, DC.

United States Environmental Protection Agency. (2025). Summary of the Occupational Safety and Health Act. Washington, DC.

University of South Florida. (2021). Portside Maintenance and Repair Reduces Workplace Hazards with Help from USF SafetyFlorida. Tampa.

University of South Florida. (2023a). SafetyFlorida: Overview. Tampa.

University of South Florida. (2023b). SafetyFlorida Consultation Program. Tampa.

University of South Florida. (2023c). About Us. Tampa.

Zuboff, Shoshana. (2021). A era do capitalismo de vigilância. São Paulo: Intrínseca.

Made in the USA
Monee, IL
04 November 2026

67377503R00085